THE SOCIAL LAWS OF THE QORÂN

THE SOCIAL LAWS OF THE QORÂN

Considered, and compared with those of the Hebrew and other ancient codes

BY

ROBERT ROBERTS

B.A.(Wales), Ph.D.(Leip.)

CURZON PRESS

First published London 1925
New Edition 1971
Curzon Press Ltd · London and Dublin

SBN 7007 0009 9

Printed in Offset by Kingprint Limited
Richmond, Surrey, England.

THIS WORK IS DEDICATED

TO THE MEMORY OF THE LATE

REV. THOMAS WITTON DAVIES

B.A., PH.D., D.D., M.R.A.S.

A GREAT TUTOR, AND A TRUE AND GENEROUS FRIEND, IN GRATEFUL ACKNOWLEDGMENT OF HELP ABLY AND WILLINGLY GIVEN, IN COLLEGE DAYS AND AFTER.

PREFACE

THE following Thesis was originally written in German, and presented to the University of Leipzig according to the rule requiring that such a dissertation shall be presented and accepted before the candidate is allowed to proceed to the examination prescribed for the degree of Doctor of Philosophy. The work gave every satisfaction to the examiners, and was marked "Admodum Laudabili."

Subsequently a section of the work was published in a series of Semitic Studies (Leipziger Semitistische Studien, ii, 6) under the title, "Das Familien,—Sklaven,—und Erbrecht im Qorân" (Leipzig: J. C. Hinrichs'sche Buchhandlung, 1908). In translating the whole Thesis into English the author took pains to examine it carefully, correcting and supplementing it wherever he deemed this possible or desirable in the light of further knowledge.

The publication of the work has been greatly delayed through the outbreak of the Great War, and the consequent enhanced cost of production. The upheaval caused by the war in Muhammedan (as well as in Christian) countries has undoubtedly changed some customs dealt with in this treatise, as, for instance, the one relating to marriage, a law having been lately passed in Turkey with the object of abolishing polygamy. But this does not affect the author's plan, which was to set out in a systematic manner the teaching of Muhammed himself as given in his book, tracing his enactments where possible to their sources; and the changes we notice are to be regarded as the result of that evolution which time and its vicissitudes produce in the social and religious customs of all peoples.

My indebtedness to the late Dr. T. Witton Davies, Bangor, I express in the dedication. My warmest thanks are also due to Drs. August Fischer and Heinrich Zimmern, Leipzig, and this I endeavour to show in my devotion to studies which are so near to their hearts, and which they have done so much to promote.

ROBT. ROBERTS.

TREFNANT, NORTH WALES,
September, 1924.

CONTENTS

APPENDICES

THE SOCIAL LAWS OF THE QORÂN

INTRODUCTION

In the whole history of the human race it would be difficult to find a character that possesses such different elements as that of the founder of Islâm. Whilst admiring his many noble qualities, his uprightness, his simplicity, his unselfishness, and his affability, qualities which undoubtedly accounted more or less for the success of his mission; yet one is constantly brought face to face with facts, and reminded of enactments and of fictitious revelations which must make the task of his defenders against those who stamp him as an impious impostor a most difficult one. Such is the man whose social system we have in this treatise to consider.

And what is true of the man, is equally true of his system (if, indeed, we may speak of a system). And naturally so. His strength and his weakness are reflected in his laws. That he did much to abolish unjust practices and cruel customs, and so to better the condition of the poor and the oppressed, and to secure to widows and orphans their just rights, no one can deny. On the other hand, we find side by side with these beneficent enactments, others which, owing especially to their stereotyped character, must, we believe, sooner or later prove the undoing of Islâm.

In the following pages we shall consider the social laws of Islâm as they are given in the Qorân, with regard to their character, and, as far as possible and desirable, as to their sources. In some cases it will be necessary, or at any rate well, to refer more fully to the works of the different Muhammedan schools, as, for instance, in the case of theft, which Muhammed has dismissed with one short reference. But in general we shall confine ourselves to the simple teaching of the Qorân itself.

As regards the sources of these Muslim laws, several things must be borne in mind. Much has been written on Muhammed's debt to Judaism, perhaps too much.[1] That the prophet could have borrowed from Judaism, and, in fact, has done so very freely, has already been clearly shown by Geiger.[2] But, on the other hand, it must not be thought that mere resemblance is in every case a proof of borrowing. There may be strong presumption; but that is all that can be said. There are many customs which are common to all Eastern nations, and cannot be traced to the code of any particular people; while other customs again obtain among most primitive people, whether of East or West, as, for instance, that of retaliation. We must also find out in what forms these customs existed among the Arabs of pre-Islâmic times. For Muhammed appeared as a social reformer no less than as the founder of a religion. And so the direction which his reforms took was naturally determined by the character of the practices which obtained in Arabia at the time of his appearance.

Further, some measure of originality must certainly be allowed to Muhammed himself. The founder of Islâm is often charged with the want of originality, and, no doubt, the charge is to some extent well-founded. But the fact that the laws of the Qorân show a marked resemblance to many of those found in the Old Testament and Talmudic literature should not prevent us from giving him the credit for original enactments when we

[1] See E. Deutsch's lecture on Islâm in his "Literary Remains"; also R. Bosworth Smith, "Mohammed and Mohammedanism," § 3.

[2] In "Was hat Mohammed aus dem Judenthume aufgenommen?" Bonn, 1833. Cf. also Fleischer, "Das Arabische" in Geiger's "Preisschrift, Kl. Schriften" II. 107 ff.

meet with them. And that such enactments are found in the social system of Islâm will be clearly seen from the following pages.[1]

We have said that the character of Muhammed's reforms was determined by the customs of his own time. It will be well, therefore, to say a few words here on the constitution of Arabic society.

The Arabs were divided into two classes, namely, those who dwelt in the desert, and those who dwelt in towns and villages. The former were nomads, inhabiting a part of the Higâz, and especially the Nagd, and roaming about from place to place within their territory, in order to secure the best pasturage for their camels, sheep, horses, etc. They preserved almost intact the manners, customs, and primeval simplicity of the early patriarchs, dwelling in their tents of hair or woollen cloth. The other class, those of the towns, were much more advanced in civilization.[2] They were occupied in agriculture and trade; and their caravans set out regularly in summer and winter either for Palestine and the chief towns of Syria, or for south Arabia.[3]

These two chief groups were again divided into a number of smaller groups. W. R. Smith says:[4] "The Arabs throughout the peninsula formed a multitude of local groups, held together within themselves not by any elaborate political organisation but by a traditional sentiment of unity, which they believed or feigned to be a unity of blood, and by the recognition and exercise of certain mutual obligations and social duties and rights.

[1] See E. H. Palmer, "The Qur'an" (= "The Sacred Books of the East," ed. by F. Max Müller, vols. vi and ix), part i., Introd. liii f.

[2] It is becoming more and more clear (says Prof. Fischer) that the Bedouins also in certain parts of pre-Islamic Arabia, especially in the Nagd and Higâz, as well as in the northern borderlands, possessed a higher culture than is commonly attributed to them. Also in the Sahara of the present day are some tribes which are not without some education. He also refers to the Šingît in Adrar as well as the علماء and says that in Marocco not only the men but also many of the women and children are able to read and write.

[3] See Sûra, chap. 106, and the commentaries thereon.

[4] "Kinship and Marriage in Early Arabia," new ed., p. 1 ff.

. . . According to the theory of the Arab genealogists the groups were all patriarchal tribes, formed by subdivision of an original stock, on the system of kinship through male descents. A tribe was but a larger family; the tribal name was the name, or nickname, of the common ancestor. . . . Between a nation, a tribe, a sept or sub-tribe, and a family there is no difference, on this theory, except in size and distance from the common ancestor."

The two most important social groups were the tribe and the clan, that is, the largest and the smallest divisions, with other divisions of less importance between them. These two divisions formed likewise the two poles of the system. The tribe comprised all those families which regularly wandered about together at certain times of the year. In their wanderings they would spread out over a pretty large area, some members being often a good distance from the others. A tribe consisted of about one thousand souls; a larger number would be too great for the pasture as well as for wandering together, and consequently would have to divide itself again.

The clan, again, consisted of those families who were most nearly related by blood to each other. These always had their tents pitched quite close together in the same quarter.[1] Each clan had its own chief; and there was also a chief at the head of the whole tribe. The position held by these chiefs rested upon the free acknowledgment of their fitness for the post by reason of their personal character and their wealth.

Whatever may have been the origin of these groups, the bond of union was of the strongest character. If a man was guilty of homicide within his own group, the act was murder, and his nearest relatives did not attempt to protect him from the consequences. But when the murdered man belonged to another group, the whole group to which the slayer belonged stood by him, and

[1] See Wellhausen, "Ein Gemeinwesen ohne obrigkeit," p. 2 ff.

that even when the two groups, that of the murderer and that of the murdered, were closely related.

Such was the case also as regards blood-revenge. While the duty of securing blood-revenge fell especially upon those who were most nearly related to the slain, that is, the next of kin,[1] yet it was regarded as something which concerned the group as a whole. In the case of murder, the next of kin could accept or refuse money compensation; and whatever his decision might be, the whole group stood by him, so that when a settlement in this wise was not arrived at, it was always a case of the whole group of the slain against the whole group of the slayer.

As we have already remarked, each tribe had its chief. His position, founded upon descent, depended for its maintenance on his personal qualities. The position of a chief was by no means an easy one. He had some authority, it is true, but it was very limited, while the duties connected with the post were many and important. " Das Wort *noblesse oblige* ist bei den Arabern keine blosse Redensart, sondern volle Wahrheit." [2] The chief must be fearless and generous. His tent must be so pitched in the camp that it should be the first that the enemy attacks, and also the first that the wayward stranger sets his eyes upon. In war he must be ready to give his blood, in peace his goods. At night a fire must, if possible, be kindled near his tent, to guide the wanderer of the desert to it, where he might find shelter.[3] He is expected to support the widows and the orphans within the tribe, to feed the hungry, and to help the debtor to pay his debts.

But the Arab of the desert had faults as great and as

[1] Cf. 2 Sam. xiv, 7 ff.; also the word גֹּאֵל in the Old Testament.

[2] Wellhausen, " Ein Gemeinwesen ohne obrigkeit," p. 7.

[3] وما أُخْمِدَتْ نارٌ لَنَا دُونَ طارقٍ * ولا ذَمَّنا فى النّازلينَ نَزِيلُ " And not one of our fires was extinguished before a wanderer, neither was a guest among the guests reproved."—" Samau'al b. 'Âdijâ " (see Wright's " Reading-Book," p. 187, 1).

many as his virtues. He was given to robbery, was cruel and superstitious, and of the inhuman customs, which were practised down to Muhammed's time, we learn in old Arabic poetry as well as in the Qorân itself. Also the treatment of the defenceless, that is, of widows and orphans, was cruel and unjust in the extreme.

Before proceeding to the consideration of the several laws, a word may be said here as regards the quotations found in the work. As to the Qorân, while I naturally always had before me the Arabic text as can easily be seen, I also consulted the translations of Palmer, Rodwell, and Sale, and occasionally that of Ullmann (Bielefeld and Leipzig, 1897) and Kasimirski (Paris, 1844). I had also by me the well-known work of Sprenger, "Das Leben und die Lehre des Mohammad." The work of Palmer is certainly the best English translation we possess. That of Sale, on the whole, gives the sense of the original well, but is often too periphrastic. My quotations from the code of Hammurabi are taken for the most part from the German translation of Winckler (Leipzig, 1904). I also consulted those of Harper (Chicago, 1904), Johns (Cambridge, 1903), D. H. Müller (Vienna, 1903) and Kohler-Peiser (Leipzig, 1904). As regards the Old Testament, I regularly consulted the translation of Kautzsch (Freiburg and Leipzig, 1896), always, however, keeping before me the Hebrew text itself.

A. LAWS CONCERNING MARITAL RELATIONS

I. Marriage

1. *The number of legitimate wives*

Among many Eastern nations polygamy is a recognized practice, and it appears that Muhammed found no reason why he should abolish the existing custom among the Arabs. As to the number of lawful wives which a Muslim is allowed to marry, we find only one reference in the Qorân, namely in Sûra 4, 3.

> "If ye fear that ye cannot act with equity towards orphans, take in marriage of such women as please you two or three or four. But if ye fear that ye cannot act equitably (towards so many), marry one only, or the slaves which ye shall have acquired."

Although one cannot say that the above words as to the number of wives allowed are very clear, especially having regard to the fact that it is the only reference made to the matter in the Qorân, still, it is the general opinion of Muhammedan scholars that a believer may marry four wives, and no more, but that there is no restriction whatever as to the number of concubines which a man may have. Certain scholars of the Shi'a maintain, however, that besides four wives permanently married, a man may contract several temporary marriages. But the Sunnites and the Mu'tazilites regard such a practice as immoral.[1]

In the Durrat al-ĝawwâs of Hariri (A.D. 1054–1122) Thorbecke's ed. μf, we find the following tradition:

[1] See Syed Ameer Ali, "The Personal Law of the Mahommedans," p. 246 f.

" The prophet said to Gailân, when he became a Muslim, and there were to him ten wives, Choose four of these, and separate thyself from the rest." [1]

This is but one of many passages, which, at least according to tradition,[2] show in unmistakable terms how polygamy was sanctioned by Islâm's legislator.

No words can adequately express the great and many evils of polygamy, bringing, as it does, in its train the most degrading consequences to both sexes alike. However, in treating of polygamy among the Muslims, we must always bear in mind the fact that there is a great difference between sanctioning and originating or introducing a system. And in fairness to Muhammed it must be said that he limited rather than introduced the practice among the Arabs. As we have already remarked, polygamy was the rule among the Eastern peoples before Muhammed's time; and so also among the Arabs; Muhammed found it practised with unbounded licence from immemorial times. And not only Muhammed himself, but also all his followers were polygamists. Therefore, in allowing polygamy Muhammed was following the general Arabic custom. Also, the prophet had before him the precedent of Jewish polygamy. In the Old Testament he would find many examples of polygamy in the history of the patriarchs, kings and others, and that without any express reprehension of a higher power. That Muhammed had not himself read the Old Testament is almost certain; still in an indirect way he was acquainted with a large part of it.[3] Perhaps also, as Sale remarks,[4] in placing a limit to polygamy, Muhammed was influenced by the decision of the Jewish doctors, who,

[1] This report is found also in the biographical works, as, for instance, in Nawawi's " Biogr. Dict.," ed. by Wüstenfeld.

[2] " Die ' Überlieferung ' spiegelt allerdings, wie namentlich Goldziher gezeigt hat, mit historischer Treue im allgemeinen nur die Verhältnisse wider, wie sie sich erst nach dem Tode des Prophetén allmählich in der muslimischen Gemeinde herausgestellt haben."—A. Fischer.

[3] See Geiger, " Was hat Mohammed aus dem Judenthume aufgenommen," p. 23 ff.

[4] Sale, " Koran," Prel. Discourse, § 6.

by the way of counsel, limit the number of wives to four, though their law confines them not to any certain number.[1]

It may well be asked whether Muhammed recognized the evils of polygamy. We do not think so. At any rate, other men, standing on a higher plane of civilization than Muhammed, have failed to recognize them, or else did not wish to do so. Hallam[2] points out that the German reformers, even so late as the sixteenth century, admitted the validity of a second or third marriage contemporaneously with the first, in default of issue and other similar causes. And Schopenhauer three centuries later praises the Mormons because they have made converts by throwing off what he terms "the unnatural bondage of monogamy." Similar sentiments may be found in the works of Eduard von Hartmann, who observes that the natural instinct of man is in favour of polygamy, and that of woman in favour of monogamy.[3] Bearing these things in mind, one need not be surprised that Muhammed, an Arab of the seventh century, could not see the evils of polygamy, and so made no attempt to abolish it.

Moreover, it is very questionable whether the prophet could have abolished polygamy entirely had he wished to do so. One is reminded of Solon's words to the Greeks, that his laws were not the best that he could devise, but that they were the best they could receive. Great as was Muhammed's influence, we believe that it would have been absolutely impossible for him to abolish the custom of polygamy among such a people. What he could do, he did. If he could not abolish, he could and did restrict. He enacted, as Sûra 4, 3 shows, that no man should marry more wives than he could adequately provide for. And this command is generally observed,

[1] The Karaites, however, did not recognize the validity of any limitation. See Syed Ameer Ali, "The Personal Law of the Mahommedans," p. 26.

[2] "Constitutional History of England," Vol. I., p. 68. See Appendix 4.

[3] See "Philosophie des Unbewussten," 3 Aufl., Berlin, 1871, p. 201.

since one wife is the rule among the poorer classes, nor is it by any means confined to these alone.[1]

2. *Concubines*

In addition to the four legal wives which the Qorân allows to a Muhammedan, he is also permitted to cohabit with his female slaves. In this case nothing is said as to number; they are allowed to him without any restriction whatever. Sûra 70, 29 ff. reads :—

> "And those who abstain from the carnal knowledge of women, other than their wives or those which their right hands possess; for as to them they shall be blameless. But whoever coveteth any women besides these, they are transgressors." [2]

This is a Meccan Sûra, and is ascribed by Muir [3] to the period before the Abyssinian migration. This, then, would appear to be the first official permission given to cohabitation with female slaves, and is one of the earliest compromises by which the prophet fitted his system to the usages and wants of those about him. This permission naturally furnished a strong inducement to his followers to fight the battles of Islâm, since the women taken captive in battle would become lawful concubines to their captors.

These female slaves are usually referred to as "That which your right hands possess." [4] In the beginning of Islâm they would consist almost entirely of those women or girls taken in war. But they might also be purchased, gifted, or in any other way acquired. And as the passages in the Qorân show, a man may acquire and

[1] In a letter to me Mr. J. D. Bryan, Alexandria, says, "In the towns the better class Moslems *as a rule* have only one wife at a time. In the country districts they have two or three, seldom four. A wife is useful to the *fellah*, and a source of revenue, for she can help in field-work, etc."

[2] See also Sûras 4, 28; 23, 5; 33, 50, etc.

[3] "The Corân, Its Composition and Teaching," p. 43.

[4] مَا مَلَكَتْ أَيْمَانُكُمْ.

cohabit with as many as he pleases, and that without there being any obligations attaching to marriage.

The slave is entirely at the will of her master, and may be sold again by him at any moment. On the other hand, it is forbidden by Muslim law to cast out a slave when she has given birth to a child;[1] and if it be a son, it is the rule, at least in some lands, to give the mother her freedom, following the precedent of Muhammed and Mary the Copt.[2]

Although, however, polygamy is sanctioned, and cohabitation with female slaves without any restriction allowed by the Qorân, one must not think that advantage of this degrading practice is taken by the generality of Muslims. As we have already seen, among the poorer classes especially one wife is the rule. As regards polygamy in India, for instance, Syed Ameer Ali says:[3] "A custom has grown up in that country, which is largely followed by all classes of the community, of drawing up a marriage deed containing a formal renunciation on the part of the future husband of any right or semblance of right which he might possess or claim to possess to contract a second marriage during the existence of the first. This custom serves as a most efficacious check upon the growth and perpetuation of the institution of polygamy. In India more than ninety-five per cent. of Mahommedans are at the present moment, either by conviction or necessity, monogamists." The author further refers to the statement of Colonel Macgregor that in Persia only two per cent. of the population enjoy the questionable luxury of plurality of wives.

3. *Impediments to Marriage*

Having considered the question as to how many wives or concubines a Muslim is allowed to take to himself,

[1] The legal term for such a slave is أُمّ الوَلَد. On the death of her master, a أم الولد, together with her children, become free.

[2] Cf. Lane, "Modern Egyptians," p. 116, and Muir, "The Corân," p. 58.

[3] "The Personal Law of the Mahommedans," p. 29.

we have next to ask whom, according to the Qorân, it is lawful to him to marry; that is, how far (*a*) Blood-relationship, and (*b*) Religion is a bar to marriage among the Muhammedans.

(a) *Blood-relationship, or Consanguinity.*—Among the ancients generally the marriage laws and customs were very lax. With the Egyptians it was lawful to marry sisters and half-sisters. Among the Persians marriage was allowed with a mother, daughter, and sister. And the same is said to have been the case among the Medians, Indians, Ethiopians, as well as the Assyrians.[1] On the other hand, the Greeks and Romans abhorred such marriages. Among the Athenians and Spartans marriages with half-sisters only were allowed. "The profane lawgivers of Rome," says Gibbon,[2] "were never tempted by interest or superstition to multiply the forbidden degrees; but they inflexibly condemned the marriage of sisters and brothers, hesitated whether first cousins should be touched by the same interdict, revered the parental character of aunts and uncles, and treated affinity and adoption as a just imitation of the ties of blood."

The Arabs before the time of Muhammed were in this respect very strict, and would not allow of a marriage with a mother, daughter, or aunt, maternal or paternal, or with two sisters at the same time. The only cases on record of marriage between brothers and sisters among the Arabs are among the inhabitants of Mirbât, referred to by Seetzen.[3] But W. R. Smith [4] thinks that Seetzen means marriage between men and their half-sisters. We will now see what the Qorân itself says on the subject.

Sûra 4, 26 ff. "Marry not women whom your fathers have married; for this is a shame and hateful, and an evil way. Though what is past may be allowed.[5] Forbidden to you are your mothers,

[1] See Keil on Lev., chap. 18.
[2] "Roman Empire," Vol. 3, p. 230.
[3] See Keil, Lev., chap. 18.
[4] "Kinship and Marriage," p. 192.
[5] What took place in the Time of Ignorance, previous to the revelation of the Qorân, would be forgiven to them.

> and your daughters, and your sisters, and your aunts, both on the father and mother's side, and your nieces on the brother and sister's side, and your foster-mothers, and your foster-sisters, and the mothers of your wives, and your step-daughters, who are your wards, born of such wives to whom you have gone in; but if ye have not gone in unto them, it shall be no sin in you (to marry them); and the wives of your sons who proceed out of your loins. And ye may not have two sisters at the same time, except where it is already done. Verily God is indulgent and graceful. Forbidden to you also are married women,[1] except those whom your right hands possess. This is the law of God for you; whatever is besides this is allowed to you."

From these verses we see that Muhammed forbids the marriage of a person with the following relations, (*a*) mother,[2] (*b*) daughter,[3] (*c*) sister, (*d*) aunt, (*e*) niece, (*f*) foster-mother, (*g*) foster-sister, (*h*) mother-in-law, (*i*) step-daughter (conditionally), (*j*) daughter-in-law, (*k*) two sisters at the same time.

Sûra 24, 31. "Say to the believing women that they refrain their looks, and observe continence, and that they display not their ornaments,[4] except what must of necessity appear; and that they draw their veils over their bosoms, and display not their ornaments, except to their husbands, or their fathers, or their husbands' fathers, or their sons, or their husbands' sons, or their brothers,

[1] المحصنات. The meaning of this expression is by no means clear. It may be taken to mean originally, "A woman who through marriage guards herself against temptation, seduction, etc. It includes, on the one hand, the idea of marriage, and on the other that of chastity. In law *muḥṣan*, so far as it has to do with marriage, signifies those men and women who are of full age, in the full possession of their mental faculties, are free, and have practised cohabitation in a legal marriage. See Snouck Hurgronje's discussion of Sachau's Muh. Recht. in the "ZDMG.," 53. p. 161 ff. Also the Qorân Commentaries and Lexicons.

[2] And her ascendants.

[3] And her descendants.

[4] That is, their bodily charms.

or their brothers' sons, or their sisters' sons, or their women, or their female slaves," etc.[1]

It will be seen that these prohibitions agree in general with those set down in the Old Testament.[2] We notice, however, that whereas marriage with a niece is allowed in the Old Testament, it is forbidden by Muhammed. Also, we see that those whom Muhammed permits to see their near relations unveiled are precisely those to whom intermarriage is forbidden by the Hebrew lawgivers. That Muhammed was acquainted with these Old Testament laws, though perhaps only indirectly, no one can deny.

As regards the punishment for the transgressions of these laws, it will be seen that in the Old Testament disregard of these prohibitions is threatened with the most severe penalties. In the Qorân, on the other hand, nothing is said as to punishment. It is true that such marriages as are referred to by Muhammed are regarded by him as an uncleanness, an abomination, and an evil way. But beyond saying this, he does not go.

(b) *Religion.*—We notice here that the prophet makes a clear distinction between a marriage with a Jew or Christian and a marriage with an unbeliever. As regards the first, we read as follows in Sûra 5, 7 :—

" This day it is permitted to you . . . to marry virtuous women who are believers, and also virtuous women of those who have been given the Scriptures before you, when you have provided for them their dower, living chastely with them without fornication, and not taking concubines."

The expression " those who have been given the Scriptures before you " evidently denotes the Jews and Christians, of whom the prophet frequently speaks in the

[1] See also Sûra 33, 37, where marriage is allowed with the divorced wife of an adopted son, which was forbidden in the Time of Ignorance; the reason being that an adopted son is no longer regarded as a natural son. Cf. W. Rob. Smith, " Kinship and Marriage," p. 52.

[2] Cf. Lev. 18, 6 ff and 20, 17 ff. Also Art. " Marriage," in Hastings' " Dict. of the Bible," Vol. 3, p. 262 ff.

Qorân as "the people of the book" (أهل الكتاب). It is to be observed that Muhammed does not demand that these Jewish and Christian women, whom a believer takes in marriage, should adopt the religion of Islâm, but allows them to retain their own religion.[1]

In Sûra 60, 10 Muhammed deals with the question whether his followers should marry believing women whose husbands are unbelievers, when the former flee to the Muhammedans. The verse reads :—

> "O ye Believers, when believing women come over to you as refugees, try them.[2] God best knoweth their faith. And if ye also have ascertained that they are true believers, send them not back to the unbelievers; they are not lawful for them, nor are the unbelievers lawful for these women. But return to their husbands what they have spent (for their dowers); and it shall be no crime in you that ye marry them, provided ye give them their dowers."

We have here one of the conditions of the Treaty of Hudaibiya (A.D. 628).[3] According to the terms of this treaty there was to be a general restoring of whatever had come into the possession of either party. Therefore, the Muhammedans were allowed to retain the women who had come over to them, provided they returned their dower. Having done this, they were free to marry them, without even their being previously divorced by their husbands. The mere fact that the husband was an unbeliever gave a Muhammedan the right to marry the woman.

On the other hand, the prophet continues in this Sûra :—

> "But retain not any right in the unbelieving women, but demand back what ye have spent

[1] It is known that Muhammed himself took to wife a Jewess, Safiyyah, and another, Raihanah, as his concubine, without, as far as we can gather, demanding that they should immediately renounce their own religion. But see Margoliouth, "Mohammed," p. 360 f.

[2] That is, whether they really flee to you on account of your religion, and not from an impure motive.

[3] See Nöldeke, "Geschichte des Qorâns," p. 163.

(for their dowers), and let them demand back what they have spent. . . . And when wives escape from you to the unbelievers, and ye succeed in turn,[1] then give those whose wives have gone away the like of what they have spent (for their dowers)."

(c) *A Man and his Female Slaves.*—The owner of a female slave may either take her to wife or as a concubine, even when her husband is still alive, and no divorce has taken place. Sûra 4, 28 reads :—

" Forbidden to you also are virtuous (married) women,[2] except those whom your right hands possess."

According to these words it is not permissible to marry a free married woman, as long as no lawful divorce has taken place (except in the case referred to in the Treaty of Hudaibiya). On the other hand, one may take to wife a married female slave (taken in war, etc.), or take her for a concubine, even when her husband is alive, and has not divorced her. Abu Hanîfa, however, holds it to be unlawful to marry those female slaves who together with their husbands have been taken captive.[3] Also, according to Muhammedan law, a man cannot marry his own slave without having previously set her free. And this holds good also in the case of a woman in relation to a male slave. Further, the marriage of a free person with a female slave who belongs to another, is dissolved, as soon as he himself becomes her owner, and cannot be renewed except by emancipation, and a regular legal contract.[4]

As regards marriage with female slaves we may compare Deut. 21, 10 ff. The author here, however, says nothing as to the treatment of female slaves who are married when taken captive. And as, according to Deut. a man must

[1] See note in Sale's " Koran," *ad. loc.*
[2] See note, p. 13.
[3] See Baidawi on above words.
[4] Lane, " Modern Egyptians," chap. 3, p. 116.

wait a certain period, that is, one full month, before he takes his captive to wife, so also, according to Muhammedan law, must a Muslim allow a certain time to pass after acquiring a female slave before taking her as his concubine.[1]

4. *Marriage with Unchaste Persons*

On this matter we quote the following words from Sûra 24, 3:—

> " The adulterer shall not marry other than an adulteress or an idolatress; and an adulteress shall not marry other than an adulterer or an idolater. Such marriages are forbidden to the believers."

Some maintain that this command refers only to the poorer Muhâgirûn, who would marry the unchaste women of the unbelievers, in order that they might earn money by means of them. Others, however, hold the command to be of universal application. But all are agreed that the command has been abrogated by the words, " Marry those among you who are single (Sûra 24, 32).[2] We may also compare the following words in verse 26 of the same Sûra:

> " Bad women for bad men, and bad men for bad women; virtuous women for virtuous men, and virtuous men for virtuous women."

To the word الخَبِيث fem. الخَبِيثة which we translate " bad " Lane [3] gives the meanings, " bad, corrupt, hated, abominable "; and he says further: " It is applied to objects of the senses and to those of the intellect; to sustenance or victuals, and to offspring, and men . . . and you apply this epithet to adultery or fornication." That the word in the above quotation refers to adultery or

[1] It is generally one to three months. See Lane as above, also Sachau, " Muh. Recht nach Schafiitischer Lehre," § 17, 87 ff. The usual legal term for this is الاستبراء.

[2] See the commentaries of Baidawi and Galâlain.

[3] Lexicon.

fornication is clear from the connection, where the prophet deals with those who accuse virtuous women of fornication. The matter arose in connection with the suspicion concerning Ayeshah occasioned by her sudden return from the expedition against Muṣṭaliq.[1]

Although nothing on this subject is to be found in the Old Testament, with the exception of the command concerning the priests;[2] still one may say that the whole spirit of this book is set against such a procedure as it is put in Sûra 24, 3. Also in Josephus we find the following words :—

> " No man ought to marry a harlot, whose matrimonial oblations, arising from the prostitution of her body, God will not accept." [3]

When we make every allowance for the time in which Muhammed lived, and especially for the sensuous character of the people for whom he had to legislate, still his marriage laws, when placed side by side with those of other legislators compare very unfavourably. For example, one would look in vain in the code of Hammurabi[4] for such licences as are granted by Muhammed to his followers. The defenders of Islâm refer triumphantly to the absence of prostitutes in Muhammedan countries. But it will be clearly seen that such a class can very well be wanting where an unbounded licence to cohabit with female slaves is granted, and where, as we shall show in the following section, the procuring of a divorce is a mere matter of form.

II. Divorce

The subject of divorce is one that occupies much space on the pages of the Qorân; and one may say that scarcely any part of the social system of Islâm is so unsatisfactory

[1] On this affair see Margoliouth, " Mohammed," pp. 340 ff.

[2] Lev. 21, 7, 14 f. : " They shall not take a woman that is a harlot, or profane; neither shall they take a woman put away from her husband; for he is holy unto his God. . . . A widow, or one divorced, or a profane woman, an harlot, these shall he not take," etc.

[3] " Antiquities," Bk. IV, chap. 8.

[4] See § 144 ff.

and condemnable as this. While granting that a law of divorce was absolutely necessary, that divorce, like polygamy, was a custom of the Arabs which Muhammed could not have abolished, still the facility with which a divorce might be procured cannot, on any ground whatever, be justified. In treating this subject we shall remark upon the following points :—

1. *The grounds of divorce.*
2. *The repetition of divorce.*
3. *The treatment of divorced women.*

1. *The Grounds of Divorce.*—If we were considering the law of divorce as it is found on the statute books of European countries, we would have to consider the question as it affects the wife as well as the husband. But in Islâm, at least as far as the teaching of the Qorân goes, the right of divorce is confined entirely to the husband, and anything beyond this must be looked for in the works of the Muhammedan jurists, who, it must be admitted, have to some extent made up for the one-sided treatment of the subject by the prophet.

We have already referred to the necessity for a law of divorce in general. With the Arabs, as indeed with Eastern peoples generally, the need of such a law was much greater than it is with us, since their social relations are so very different from ours. This need arises especially from the separation of the sexes, and in connection with this the practice among women of wearing the veil. Formerly it was thought that the use of the veil by women was first introduced by Muhammed; and for this he has been much reproached. This, however, was a mistake, for the veil was used in Arabia long before the time of the prophet.[1] However, Muhammed retained it as a means of separation between the sexes. What we have here is another instance of a man perpetuating rather than

[1] See esp. Snouck Hurgronje, "Twee populaire dwalingen" (Sonderabdr. aus den Bijdragen tot de Taal-Land-en Volkenkunde usf. 5e Volgr. I), p. 10 ff.

introducing a custom. When we now consider this separation of the sexes, and how thus a man may marry a woman whom he has never seen, one can easily understand how such a man may afterwards be anxious to free himself from his wife, and how also a divorce may be necessary for the happiness of the parties thus joined together, as well as for the sake of morality and the prevention of more grievous sins. Further, it will be seen that here also, as in the case of polygamy, the prophet had before him the precedent of the Old Testament Scriptures, to which we shall again refer. On the other hand, the great facility with which a man may divorce his wife; the fact that any trivial cause is sufficient to secure for a Muslim his freedom, naturally weakens the marriage bond, and reduces woman to the most degrading position in the social scale.[1]

That a Muhammedan may put away his wife from mere dislike, and without assigning any reason whatsoever for his action, may be seen from the following passages. Sûra 2, 226 f. :—

> "Those who vow to separate themselves from their wives shall have four months to consider it. If they recall their vow, God is gracious and merciful. But if they resolve on a divorce, verily God heareth and knoweth it."

Also v. 228 f. :—

> "The men stand over them (the women). . . . Ye may divorce your wives twice. After that ye must either retain them with kindness, or put them away with liberality."

Also v. 237 :—

> "It shall be no crime in you if ye divorce your wives so long as ye have not consummated the marriage, nor have settled any dowry on them. But

[1] "Your remarks about the facility of divorce and its consequences are only too true, as a residence in a Mohammedan country convinces one."—Prof. A. H. Sayce, M.A., LL.D.

> provide for them, the rich and the poor according to his means, in a becoming manner, a compensation."

Sûra 4, 24 :—

> "If ye desire to exchange one wife for another, and have given one of them a good sum,[1] make no deduction from it."

Although the prophet in these passages speaks against the showing of inconsiderate haste in the case of divorcing a wife, as well as against any harsh treatment of her, when a man has finally decided on a divorce, still is the greatest freedom allowed to him. As to the ground of divorce, not a word is said. We simply read that "the men stand over the women"; and whenever they will, have they the right to free themselves from them, without any other cause than a mere desire to exchange one wife for another.

It must not be assumed, however, that the Muhammedans in general avail themselves of this fatal facility of divorce. Sale says[2] that "They are seldom known to proceed to the extremity of divorce, notwithstanding the liberty given them, it being reckoned a great disgrace so to do." On the other hand, Lane, while using words much of the same import as the above quoted from Sale, in "The Manners and Customs of the Modern Egyptians," still shows clearly enough that, in certain parts, at least, this liberty is very fully taken advantage of. He says :— "There are many men in this country who in the course of ten years have married as many as twenty, thirty, or more wives; and women not far advanced in age who have been wives to a dozen or more men successively. I have heard of men who have been in the habit of marrying a new wife almost every month."[3] Writing of earlier

[1] That is a قِنْطَار (see Lane, Lexicon, under the word). Muhammed means, "Be it ever so great."

[2] "Koran," Prel. Discourse, chap. 6.

[3] Chap. 6, p. 192. The fact as to the frequency of divorce is also proved by Snouck Hurgronje in Bk. 2 of his "Mekka."

times, the same author, in "Arabian Society in the Middle Ages" (ed. by Stanley Lane-Poole, Chatto and Windus, 1883), says: "It is the opinion of most persons, I believe, among the more strictly religious, that a man may not have more than four women, whether they be wives alone, or concubine slaves alone, or of both classes together; but the practice of some of the companions of the Prophet, who cannot be accused of violating his precepts, affords a strong argument to the contrary. 'Alee, it is said, was the most devout of the companions; but he had four wives and seventeen concubines besides, and married, after Fáṭimeh (may God be well pleased with her!), among all that he married and divorced, more than two hundred women; and sometimes he included four wives in one contract, and sometimes divorced four at one time, taking other four in their stead." [1]

I may also quote here from a letter, already referred to, which I recently received from Mr. J. D. Bryan, Alexandria. He says: "It is impossible to get reliable statistics on the question of divorce here in Egypt. The system is so slack, and divorce so easy. . . . Divorce is *very* common, both in the towns and country districts. Dr. Watson, the senior American missionary in Cairo, once said that 95 per cent. of the Moslem marriages resulted in divorce. When I saw this statement I made inquiries amongst my Moslem friends, and found that there cannot have been much exaggeration, if any, in this figure. In only two cases did I find men, amongst those I inquired of or about, who had retained their wives or wife till death."

But whether Muhammedans avail themselves of this right or not, the liberty to do so always remains; and a man who may exchange his wives ever so often, can always appeal to the Qorân in justification of his act. And it is just here that the evil comes in. A system where the wife has continually hanging over her head the apprehension of divorce cannot but prove an abiding source of uneasiness to her. It is an intolerable system, and con-

[1] P. 222. See also p. 224.

sistent only with that social degradation of the female sex which is its inseparable attendant.

Further, we notice the one-sidedness of this freedom of divorce. While the husband has the right to dissolve the marriage tie whenever he desires, and for any trivial cause, no such privilege is allowed to the wife. True, she can claim, according to Muhammedan law, to be released from her husband, but not even here without some real cause of complaint, such as cruel treatment or neglect; [1] and even concerning such cases not a word is said by the prophet himself in the Qorân.

However, it must be admitted that what we read on this subject in the Qorân is not very different from what one will find in the legal codes of the ancients generally, and even modern civilization has not attained to a recognition of the equality of the sexes in this matter. The Old Testament recognizes only the right of the husband to divorce; and for a time, at least, in the history of the Romans, " the slavery of the wretched female was hopeless and perpetual unless the husband asserted for his own convenience the manly prerogative of divorce." [2]

Also as regards the cause or causes of divorce, there seems to be very little difference, if indeed any, between what is said in the Qorân from what we find in the Old Testament. Thus we read in Deut. 24, 1 :—

> " When a man taketh a wife, and marrieth her; then it shall be, if she find no favour in his eyes, because he has found some unseemly thing in her, that he shall write her a bill of divorcement, and give it in her hand, and send her out of his house."

It is not clear what the expression עֶרְוַת דָּבָר, which we translate " unseemly thing," means. Kautzsch translates " etwas Widerwärtiges " (something repulsive, disgusting). The Septuagint has ἄσχημον πρᾶγμα, and the Vulgate

[1] Also owing to the serious infirmity (mental or physical) or the impotence of the husband. See Sachau, " Muh. Recht.," p. 8 f.

[2] Gibbon, " Roman Empire," Vol. 3, p. 228.

"aliquem foetiditatem." In Guthe's "Bibelwörterbuch"[1] it is said "wahrscheinlich eine sexuelle Abnormität des Weibes, die eine fruchtbare Ehe unmöglich machte."[2]

But whatever may be the exact meaning of this expression, it is clear from the New Testament that the Jews of later times did not regard the proof of adultery as necessary for a divorce. Matt. 5, 31 f. reads :—

> "It was said also, Whosoever shall put away his wife, let him give her a writing of divorcement: but I say unto you, that every one that putteth away his wife, saving for the cause of fornication, maketh her an adulteress; and whosoever shall marry her when she is put away committeth adultery."[3]

The meaning of the expression עֶרְוַת דָּבָר was also much disputed among the old Jewish doctors. The rigid and casuistical school of Shammai taught that a man could not put away his wife unless he found something shameful in her דְּבַר עֶרְוָת, because it is said in Deut. 24, 1: "Because he has found a shameful thing in her" (עֶרְוַת דָּבָר). Shammai explained the expression ערות דבר as "rem impudicam, libidinem, lasciviam, impudicitiam." On the other hand, the more lax school of Hillel said, "Also when she burns his food," appealing to the word דבר (= anything).[4] And, says Tholuck,[5] "It is but a natural consequence of Hillelism, when R. Akiba, whose opinion is usually adduced as a third one, following the Mishna, considers any reason whatever a sufficient justification of divorce, 'even if the wife have only put too much salt into the food,' or, 'if another please me better'; and quotes the Scripture as an authority in his favour, because it is said

[1] Art. "Ehe" by Siegfried, p. 143.

[2] "Probably a sexual abnormality in the wife which makes a fruitful marriage impossible." See also Driver's "Deut." ("Inter. Crit. Comm.") on the passage.

[3] See also Mark 10, 2 ff.

[4] Cf. Matt. 19, 3, where the Pharisees ask, "Is it lawful for a man to put away his wife for every cause?"

[5] "Comm. on the Sermon on the Mount," p. 221. Also cf. Strack, "Einleitung in den Talmud³," p. 28 note, and the commentaries on Deut.

at the beginning of Deut. 24, 1 אִם־לֹא תִמְצָא־חֵן בְּעֵינָיו."
But whatever may be the precise meaning of ערות דבר it cannot refer to adultery, since according to the Old Testament adultery was to be punished with death.

What has been said on the question of divorce as far as the Old Testament and the Qorân are concerned, holds good also as regards the Hammurabi code. While the husband can put away his wife with the greatest ease, the case of the wife is totally different. A divorce in her favour is allowed only after a thorough investigation into her life previous to her application.[1] Cf. § 133 ff.

Therefore, as far as the grounds of divorce as set forth in the Qorân are concerned, there seems to be but little difference between them and those found in the codes of other eastern peoples.

2. *The Repetition of Divorce.*—As regards the number of times which a Muhammedan may divorce the same wife, the Qorân is very clear. Sûra 2, 229 f. reads :—

> " Ye may divorce your wives twice; after that ye must either retain them with kindness, or put them away with benefits. . . . (230) If then the husband divorce her (a third time), it is not lawful for him to take her again, until she shall have married another husband. And if he also divorce her, then shall no blame attach to them if they return to each other, if they think they can observe the ordinances of God."

From the above words we see that a Muhammedan may divorce his wife twice without being obliged to part with her. The ceremony of divorce among the Muhammedans is very simple, the husband merely saying, " Thou art divorced," or, " I herewith dismiss thee." [2]

[1] " If a woman hates her husband and has said, 'Thou shalt not possess me,' one shall inquire into her past what is her lack, and if she has been economical and has no vice, and her husband has gone out and greatly belittled her, that woman has no blame; she shall take her marriage portion, and go off to her father's house " (§ 142). " Die Scheidung liegt ausschliesslich in der Hand des Mannes. So war es und so blieb es im mosaischen Gesetze und im rabbinischen Rechte."—D. H. Müller, "Die Gesetze Ḥammurabis," p. 123.

[2] Or some such words. See Sachau, " Muh. Recht.," p. 54 ff.

The husband might utter these words, say, in a sudden fit of anger, but soon afterwards repent of his words, and feel a desire to retain his wife. This he is allowed to do for the second time. Then comes the strange enactment, that if a man divorce his wife a third time, it is not lawful for him to take her again, until in the interval she has been married to another person, and again divorced by such second husband. This enactment is everywhere followed. Some Muhammedan scholars, however, are of opinion that if the separation had taken place under circumstances which gave rise to the inference that both parties, at the time of disagreement, had lost their self-control, some allowance should be made in their favour, and that they should be allowed to remarry without the wife having to undergo the ordeal of a marriage with another man.[1]

Here, if anywhere in Muhammed's social system, have we an enactment which is entirely peculiar. While the majority of his decrees which deal with the matter of divorce have their parallels in other systems, these referring to the possibility of repeated marriages, and the conditions attached thereto, are wholly different from what we find in other social codes and especially from the enactments found in the Old and New Testaments. Let us again look at Deut. 24, 1 ff. :—[2]

> "When a man taketh a wife, and marrieth her, then it shall be, if she find no favour in his eyes, because he hath found some unseemly thing in her, that he shall write her a bill of divorcement, and give it in her hand, and send her out of his house.

[1] See Syed Ameer Ali, "The Personal Law of the Mahommedans," p. 259. Naturally there are various dodges for avoiding the necessity for the wife to cohabit with this second or intermediary husband. See, for example, Sachau, "Muh. Recht.," p. 67.

[2] Driver ("Inter. Crit. Comm.") takes vv. 1–3 as protasis, stating the conditions of the case contemplated, and v. 4 as apodosis. He says: "The law is thus not, properly speaking, a law of divorce; the right of divorce is assumed, as established by custom (comp. Chap. 22, vv. 19, 29, two cases in which the right is forfeited); but definite legal formalities are prescribed, and restrictions are imposed, tending to prevent its being lightly or rashly exercised." See also Appendix 5.

(2) And when she is departed out of his house, she may go and be another man's *wife.* (3) And if the latter husband hate her, and write her a bill of divorcement, and give it in her hand, and send her out of his house; or if the latter husband die, which took her to be his wife; (4) her former husband, which sent her away, may not take her again to be his wife, after that she is defiled." [1]

Also Jer. 3, 1, reads :—

" If a man put away his wife, and she go from him, and become another man's, shall he return unto her again? Shall not that land be greatly polluted? But thou hast played the harlot with many lovers; yet return again to me, saith the Lord."

Again, Matt. 5, 32 :—

" Whosoever shall put away his wife, saving for the cause of fornication, causeth her to commit adultery; and whosoever shall marry her that is divorced, committeth adultery."

Whether these enactments were at all times observed or not,[2] they show us, at least, in what light the matter was regarded by the lawgivers of the Old and New Testaments. And here, as observed, we find a real difference between the Jewish-Christian system and that of the Qorân. For, whereas, according to the latter, a man may again marry his divorced wife, provided in the meantime she has been married to another, from whom in turn she has been divorced, this, according to the Jewish-Christian law, is strictly prohibited. Thus we see that the one essential condition to be complied with before remarriage with a former husband is possible according to Muhammedan law, is that which, according

[1] " The union of a divorced woman with another man, from the point of view of her first husband, falling into the same category as adultery, to which this term is applied (Lev. 18, 20, Num. 5, 13, 14, 20)."—Driver, Comm. " The marriage of a divorced woman is thus treated implicitly as tantamount to adultery, and the way is prepared for the teaching of Christ on the subject of marriage."—Keil, Comm.

[2] See Guthe, " Bibelwörterbuch," p. 143.

to Biblical law, makes remarriage a transgression. Still, it will be observed that as far as the words of the Old Testament are concerned, there is nothing to prevent a man from remarrying his divorced wife provided that in the meantime she has not been wedded to another.

3. *The Treatment of Divorced Women.*—As compensation, to a certain extent, for the wrong to which a woman is exposed, owing to the great power in the matter of divorce which the husband possesses, Islâm's legislator has laid down certain conditions which are to be observed when a separation has been decided upon. Owing to the number and importance of these conditions, it will be necessary to quote somewhat largely from the Qorân, after which we shall make a few general observations.

Sûra 2, 231 :—" When ye divorce your wives, and they have fulfilled their prescribed time,[1] either retain them with humanity, or dismiss them with kindness. But retain them not with violence. He who doth so, harmeth himself."

Sûra 2, 232 :—" When ye have divorced your wives, and they have fulfilled their prescribed time, hinder them not from marrying their (new) husbands, when they have agreed among themselves according to what is honourable."

Sûra 2, 237 f. :—" It shall be no crime in you if ye divorce your wives, so long as ye have not touched them, nor settled any dowry on them. But grant unto them, the rich and the poor, each according to his circumstances, in a becoming manner, a compensation, as is the duty of people who would act righteously. (238) And if ye divorce them before ye have touched them, but having already settled a dowry on them, ye shall give them half of what ye have settled, unless they, or he in whose hand the knot of marriage is, should release any part of it. And if ye release the whole, it shall approach nearer unto piety."

[1] أَجَل here means the end of the عِدَّة *i.e.*, the legal period of retirement assigned to a widow or divorced woman before she may marry again.

Sûra 33, 48 :—" O ye believers ! when ye marry women who are believers, and afterwards put them away before ye have touched them, there is no term prescribed to you to observe towards them. But compensate them, and dismiss them in a becoming manner."

Here we see that the wife from whom the husband has separated himself before the marriage has been consummated, has no specific time to observe before joining another in marriage. But the husband, who has thus divorced his wife, must grant her a compensation,[1] that is, if he has not fixed a dowry (فَرِيضة). If a dowry has been fixed, he holds back one half, and, according to the Sunna, the compensation as well.[2]

Sûra 2, 233 reads :—" Mothers [3] shall give suck to their children two full years for the father who desires the time of giving suck to be completed. And the father shall be obliged to maintain and clothe them according to what shall be reasonable. But no claim shall be made against any person beyond what he is able to meet. Neither mother nor father shall suffer on account of the child. And the same duty shall fall upon an heir.[4] But if they (the parents) choose to wean the child (before this time), by common consent, and on mutual consideration, it shall be no crime in them. And if ye have a mind to provide a nurse for the child, it shall be no crime in you, if ye pay her what has been agreed upon according to what is just."

Important also as bearing upon this subject is Sûra 65, which bears the title سُورَةُ ٱلطَّلَاق ,—Divorce. It begins thus :—

[1] Called by the jurists مُتْعَة " Id, quod dono accipit mulier repudio dimissa." " Quod uxorem aliquis ducit, tum post paucorum dierum consuetudinem dimittit."—Freytag, Lex.

[2] See Baidawi on Sûra 33, 48.

[3] The reference here is to divorced mothers.

[4] According to Galâlain, heir here means a guardian or trustee. The word as Baidawi shows is variously interpreted.

" O Prophet, when ye separate yourselves from your wives, put them away at their appointed time, and compute the time exactly. . . . Do not expel them from their house, neither let them go out, unless they be guilty of manifest uncleanness.[1] . . . Thou knowest not whether God in the meantime will bring something new to pass.[2] (2) And when the appointed time is come, either retain them with kindness, or dismiss them honourably. And take two witnesses from among you, men of integrity, and give your testimony according to the will of God. . . . (4) As to such of your wives who give no hope of menstruation,[3] if ye have doubt (as regards their true condition), let their term be three months, and likewise those who have not yet commenced with their courses. The time for those who are pregnant shall be until they are delivered of their burden. . . . (6) Allow them (the women whom ye divorce) to dwell where ye dwell, according to your means, and cause them no harm, so as to bring them to straits. And if they be pregnant, spend on them what is necessary, until they be delivered. And if they suckle their children for you, give them their hire; and come to terms with each other according to what is just. But if ye experience any difficulty in this, let another woman suckle the child for you. (7) He who has plenty shall out of his plenty expend;[4] and he whose income is scanty shall expend out of what God hath given him."

Lastly, we quote Sûra 2, 228 :—

" The divorced wives shall await three menstruations, and they shall not conceal what God has created in their bodies.[5] . . . And under these circum-

[1] That is, be proven guilty of adultery.

[2] That is, whether the husbands in the meantime may not become reconciled, and so rescind the decree of divorce.

[3] By reason of their age.

[4] For both the mother and nurse.

[5] That is, they shall tell the real truth as to their condition, whether they have their courses, or be with child, or not, and shall not attempt to deceive their husbands, lest the first husband's child should be attributed to the second.

stances their husbands should take them back, in case they should wish for a reconciliation. And the same obligations fall also upon the women, according to what is just."

From the foregoing quotations we find as follows: (*a*) A woman, when she has been divorced from her husband, must wait until she has had her courses three times before she can marry another man. If there be any doubt as to whether she is subject to them or not, she must wait three months before she is free to marry. It will clearly be seen that the object of this condition is to guard against any difficulty which might arise in the future with regard to the paternity of a child, and its right to a share in the inheritance.

(*b*) If at the end of the three months the divorced wife is found not to be with child, she is at liberty to remarry whenever and to whomsoever she pleases. On the other hand, should she be pregnant, she must wait until she is delivered. During this period of waiting she may remain in her husband's house, unless she be found guilty of manifest uncleanness. This time of waiting is called عِدَّةُ ٱلْمَرْأَةِ [1] (see p. 28, note 1).

(*c*) When a man divorces his wife before the marriage has been consummated, she is not obliged to wait any particular time. In this case the husband must grant the wife compensation, that is, if no dowry has been fixed, otherwise half the dowry. The wife may take less, or the husband may give more than this half; and the greater the agreement on this point, the greater the piety.

(*d*) If the divorced wife has a young child, she shall suckle it for two full years, and the father shall provide for both during this time. Of interest as concerning this time of sucking is also Sûra 33, 13: "And his weaning shall be in two years." Also Sûra 46, 14: "We have commanded man to show kindness towards

[1] As to other meanings to this term see Lane's Lex.

his parents. His mother beareth him (in the womb) with pain, and bringeth him forth with pain. And the space of his being carried (in the womb) and of his weaning is thirty months."

As regards the further rearing of the child there is a difference of opinion among the Muhammedan jurists,[1] and our reference to the matter shall be brief. According to the Hanafees, the mother has the right to retain her daughter until she arrives at the period of puberty; while according to the Mâlikees, Shâfïees and Hanbalees she has this right over her daughter until she is married. But when we remember the fact that in Muhammedan countries the daughters, as a rule, marry as soon as they reach marriageable age, we see that there is scarcely any difference between the teaching of the various schools on this point.

On the other hand, in the case of a boy, the Mâlikees teach that the mother has the right to retain him until he reaches the age of puberty. But according to the Shâfïees and the Hanbalees the boy can choose between his father and mother when he reaches the age of seven. If the boy decides to remain with his mother, this is allowed him until he reaches the age of puberty; after that, however, he has no choice, and he falls under the care of his father. Finally, the Hanafees teach that in the case of a boy the ḥaḍâna (care) of the mother ceases when he reaches the age of seven. The teaching of the Shâfïees we pass by.

As regards the period of waiting in the case of a divorced wife, as well as the time for giving suck to the child, a parallel is found in the teaching of the Talmud. Thus we read,—" Divorced wives may not remarry before the expiration of three months." [2] Also, "A woman shall give suck to her child two years; after that it is as

[1] See Syed Ameer Ali, "The Personal Law of the Mahommedans," p. 195 ff.: also Lane, "Modern Egyptians," p. 114.

[2] גְּרוּשׁוֹת לֹא יִנָּשְׂאוּ עַד שֶׁיִּהְיוּ לָהֶן שְׁלֹשָׁה חֳדָשִׁים Mishna, "Gebhamoth," IV, 10.

though a worm sucked." [1] It is quite evident, therefore, that Muhammed is here also influenced by the teaching of the Jewish rabbis.

Also, as regards compensating a divorced wife we may compare the teaching of Muhammed with that of Hammurabi. As we have seen, Muhammed deals with two cases, namely where there is a dowry, and also where no dowry has been fixed. With the former we compare Hammurabi, § 137, which reads :—

> " If a man has set his face to put away his concubine who has borne him children, or his wife who has granted him children, to that woman he shall return her marriage portion,[2] and shall give her the usufruct of field, garden, and goods, and she shall bring up her children," etc. (cf. also § 138).

As regards the second case, Hammurabi, § 139, reads :—

> " If there was no dowry, he shall give her one mina of silver for a divorce."

Further, as according to Muhammed the rich and the poor shall give a compensation according to their circumstances, so Hammurabi, § 140, reads :—

> " If he is a poor man, he shall give her one-third of a mina of silver."

III. Adultery and Fornication

The questions to be treated here are the following :—

I. What are the proofs required before conviction can take place?

II. What are the punishments enacted?

I. *The Proofs of Adultery*

As regards these proofs, the requirements of the Qorân are such as cannot easily be complied with; and the

[1] אִשָּׁה מֵינִיקָה אֶת־בְּנָהּ שְׁתֵּי שָׁנִים מִכָּן וְאֵילָךְ כְּיוֹנֵק שֶׁקֶץ Kethuboth 60, 1. See Geiger, "Was hat Mohammed aus dem Judenthume aufgenommen?" p. 90.

[2] See Appendix 6.

prophet no doubt enacted these as a protection against hasty or false accusations.

Sûra 4, 19 reads:—" Such of your women as commit sin through adultery,[1]—produce four witnesses from among you against them," etc.

Sûra 24, 4 f.:—" As to those who accuse honourable women (of adultery), and cannot produce four witnesses, scourge them with fourscore stripes, and accept not their testimony for ever; for such are miscreants, (5) excepting those who shall afterwards repent and amend."

Sûra 24, 6 ff.:—" Those who shall accuse their own wives (of adultery), and shall have no witnesses besides themselves,—such a one shall swear four times before God that he speaketh the truth. (7) And the fifth time shall imprecate the curse of God upon him if he be a liar. (8) And it shall avert the punishment from the wife, if she four times calls God to witness that he (her husband) is a liar, (9) and the fifth time imprecates the wrath of God upon her if her husband speaketh the truth."

The above passages teach that, (*a*) A woman accused of adultery by persons other than her own husband cannot be condemned except on the testimony of four witnesses. According to Baidawi these witnesses must be men and of the believers. And it may be said that this is a general law which holds good in all cases.[2] (*b*) If a man accuses his own wife, and has no witnesses to produce, he must himself, according to Sûra 24, advance the charge of adultery against her. This declara-

[1] On the word فاحشة Lane (Lex.) says, [An excess; an enormity; anything exceeding the bounds of rectitude] . . . anything forbidden by God. . . . Also, particularly, adultery, or fornication." The Qorân and the Law know only of that general conception of unchastity which is usually denoted by زِنًى, and therefore do not differentiate between adultery in our sense of the word and other forms of unchastity. Cf. Snouck Hurgronje, "ZDMG.," 53, p. 162 f.

[2] According to Talmudic law only free men of full age were capable of bearing witness; women and slaves were incapacitated. Cf. Bâbâ Kammâ 88a and Jos., Ant., 4, 8, 15, and note in Whiston's trans.

tion will be regarded as sufficient unless the wife make a similar declaration to the contrary, in which case she would be free. However, in such a case of double swearing, according to Muhammedan law, the wife would be expelled from her husband's bed, and could not again marry him, because, as it will easily be seen, having come to such extremities, they could not well live together afterwards. Also the child which was the subject of this double swearing would be regarded as fatherless.

It will be seen that the Qorân both in its demand for a number of witnesses as well as for the punishment of false-witnesses to a certain extent follows the teaching of the Old Testament: and it is very probable that the prophet was acquainted with these Israelitic enactments. Still, as we have already remarked, too much must not be made of this agreement, since these enactments, being so natural, may be expected in any law-book.

Regarding the number of witnesses required Deut. 17, 6 reads:—

> "At the mouth of two witnesses, or three witnesses, shall he that is to die, be put to death; at the mouth of one witness he shall not be put to death." [1]

And as, according to the Qorân, a false-accuser is to be scourged with fourscore stripes, so we read in Deut. 22, 13 ff., that if a man married a woman, and afterwards made charges against her character, and so bring her to evil repute by declaring, "I took this woman, and when I came nigh to her, I found not in her the tokens of virginity," and this charge on investigation turned out to be unfounded, then shall the elders of the city take the man and cause him to be chastised; also he shall be made to pay one hundred shekels of silver to the woman's father.

But we find here one noteworthy difference, namely, that whereas according to the Muhammedan law, after

[1] Cf. also Deut. 19, 15, etc. "One witness shall not rise up against a man for any iniquity," etc.

the double swearing already referred to, the marriage should be dissolved, Deut. 22, 19 enacts :—

> " And she shall be his wife; he may not put her away all his days." [1]

It is to be noticed also that the above passages from the Old Testament deal properly not with the adultery of a married woman, but with the unchastity of the young wife before marriage.

Finally, with the above may be compared Hammurabi, § 131 :—

> " If the wife of a man her husband has accused her, and she has not been caught in lying with another male, she shall swear by God, and shall return to her house." Cf. also § 132 ff.

II. *The Punishments Enacted for Adultery*

Here several distinctions are made, as between a married and an unmarried person, and also between a free-woman and a female slave. Such distinctions, as we shall see, are also found in the Old Testament.

It is well known that by all ancient laws adultery and fornication were most severely punished; and a like severity was not unknown in Islâm. A verse by Muhammed, which is not found in the Qorân, but which we have good reason to accept as genuine, being regarded only as abrogated, reads as follows :—

> " If a man and a woman commit adultery, stone them both to death; it is a punishment decreed by God." [2]

This " verse of stoning " (آية الرجم), although, as we have seen, wanting in the Qorân, still in law holds as binding,

[1] According to Muslim law the marriage shall be annulled when the two swearing, that of the husband and of the wife, stand opposed to each other, and so neither the guilt nor the innocence of the wife has been proved. But Deut. 22, 19, sets out the innocence of the wife as proved. And so, in spite of the husband's effort to get rid of her, she shall remain his wife, and he shall never be at liberty to divorce her.

[2] See Sale, Koran, Prel. Discourse, § 3; also Nöldeke, "Gesch. des Qorâns," p. 185 f.

since stoning is enacted as punishment in the case of real adultery. Also it will be observed that the man as well as the woman is to be punished.

> Sûra 4, 19 f. reads :—" As regards such of your women as sin through unchastity, take four witnesses against them from among you. And if they bear witness against them, imprison them (the women) in your houses, until death releases them, or God affordeth a way for them. (20) And if two of you commit a sin (through unchastity), punish them both; but if they repent and amend, let them both alone, for God is merciful."
>
> Also Sûra 24, 2 :—" The adulterer and the adulteress—scourge them both with a hundred stripes. And let not compassion prevent you from executing the decree of God. . . . And let a number of believers be witnesses of their punishment."

As will be seen, the above verses are somewhat inconsistent, and far from easy to explain. As regards Sûra 4, 20, especially, the commentators are by no means agreed. Zamahshari and Baidawi maintain that the reference is to two persons of different sex, while Galalain is of opinion that sodomy is meant. The following points appear to me to favour Galalain's contention. (*a*) That the masculine gender is used in both words. (*b*) That it is this only that accounts for the smallness of the penalty. (*c*) That the punishment of women according to the immediately preceding verse is different and much more severe.

We have already observed that the punishment for adultery among the ancients was most severe. Still the mode of punishment differed greatly in different countries. With the ancient Egyptians adultery on the part of a woman was punished with the loss of the nose,[1] but nothing is said as to the fate of the male offender.[2] On

[1] G. T. Bettany, " The World's Religions," p. 480; cf. Ezek. 23, 25.
[2] As regards the Egyptians of modern times, cf. Lane, " Modern Egyptians " (written 1833–35), p. 309 : " Drowning is the punishment now almost always inflicted, publicly, upon women convicted of

the other hand, according to the Hammurabi code, the punishment, which was death by drowning, was to be inflicted upon the male as well as the female. Both were to be bound and thrown into the water. But "if the owner of the wife would save his wife, or the king would save his subject, he may do so" (§ 129).[1]

Death is also the punishment enacted in the Israelitic Code. Cf. Deut. 22, 22 :—

> "If a man be found lying with a woman married to an husband, then they shall both of them die, the man that lay with the woman, and the woman; so shalt thou put away the evil from Israel."

> Also Lev. 20, 10 :—"And the man that committeth adultery with another man's wife, even he that committeth adultery with his neighbour's wife, the adulterer and the adulteress shall surely be put to death."

But while death is here enacted as punishment, and that the man as well as the woman was to suffer the same penalty, still nothing is said as to the manner in which it was to be carried out. The Talmudists, however, suppose it to be by strangling. Thus they made a distinction between the two expressions, "He shall be put to death," and, "His blood shall be upon him," regarding the former expression as referring to death by strangulation, and the latter death by stoning. But this view can scarcely be regarded as correct. Probably the usual punishment for adultery among the Israelites was death by stoning.[2]

---

adultery in Cairo and other large towns of Egypt, instead of that ordained by the law, which is stoning," etc. In another place (p. 208) he says: "The Felláheen of Egypt resemble the Bedawees in other respects. When a Felláhah is found to have been unfaithful to her husband, in general he or her brother throws her into the Nile, with a stone tied to her neck; or cuts her in pieces, and then throws her remains into the river." Cf. Matt. 18, 6; Jos., Ant., 14, 15, 10.

[1] This right as regards a man belongs to the king as his sovereign, and as regards a woman to her husband as her lord and possessor. See Winckler on the passage.

[2] So we read in John 8, 4 f. :—"Master, this woman hath been taken in adultery, in the very act. Now in the law Moses commanded

Next we come to the case of female slaves, who in the Qorân receive a special treatment. In Sûra 4, 29, Muhammed advises those who have not sufficient means to marry free believing women to take to wife believing female slaves. Then in verse 30 he says: "And if they, when they are married, be guilty of adultery, they shall suffer half the punishment which is appointed for the free women." What is this punishment to be? In Sûra 24, 2, Muhammed says: "The whore and the whoremonger shall ye scourge with an hundred stripes." [1]

That the prophet should make a distinction between those that are free and those that are not free is only natural and just, inasmuch as the latter have not the advantages of education, etc., which the former enjoy, and consequently do not feel the same sense of responsibility. And in this also the teaching of the Qorân agrees with that of the Old Testament, as we see from the following words in Lev. 19, 20 ff.:—

> "And whosoever lieth carnally with a woman that is a bondmaid, betrothed to an husband, and not at all redeemed, nor freedom given her; they shall be punished; [2] they shall not be put to death, because she was not free. And he shall bring his guilt offering unto the Lord, unto the door of the tent of meeting, even a ram for a guilt offering.

---

us to stone such; what then sayest thou of her?" The genuineness of this passage is very doubtful; and the law referred to is wanting in the Pentateuch, both in the Hebrew and Samaritan texts, and also in the Septuagint (see the commentaries). Also cf. Ezek. 16, 39 f., and Hos., chap. 2.

[1] According to the Sunnah law, the different passages of the Qorân which deal with the punishment of unchastity are harmonized as follows: (*a*) Unchaste free married women (always presupposing that they are of age and in possession of their mental faculties), are to be punished through stoning. (*b*) Unchaste free unmarried women are to be punished with one hundred stripes, and to be banished for one year. (*c*) Unfree women for unchastity are to receive half the punishment of the free (therefore not death, which evidently cannot be halved). (*d*) Unnatural unchastity is in all cases to be punished as unchastity in general.

[2] בִּקֹּרֶת—Ahndung. Züchtigung (requital of evil, chastisement), So Ges-Buhl and Siegfried-Stade. Ewald translates Unterscheidung (distinction).

> And the priest shall make atonement for him with the ram for the guilt offering before the Lord for his sin which he hath sinned; and he shall be forgiven for his sin which he hath sinned."

The words "they shall be punished; they shall not be put to death," probably mean that the man as well as the woman shall suffer. But what was to be the punishment for the man, we do not know. According to the Mishna,[1] the punishment of the woman consisted of forty stripes.

When we look at these enactments of Muhammed regarding the proof and punishment of adultery, and having regard to the period to which they belong, we will not find much with which we can find fault. At least they are as good as the other social laws given by the prophet. It is true that the legislator directs his attention principally to the female offender; but the same is true also of the Old Testament, as well as among all peoples where polygamy and concubinage are practised. Sexual intercourse between a married man and an unmarried woman is on the man's part only a breach of the law of chastity. To the prophet's credit also is the precaution taken by him against the possibility of false accusation, as well as the distinction which he makes between free and non-free persons.

IV. Enactments Relating to Children.

In this section we have to deal with the following matters:—

1. *The duties of parents or guardians towards children.*
2. *The duties of children towards their parents.*
3. *The law concerning adoption.*

1. *The Duties of Parents or Guardians towards Children.*

One of the most commendable things which one finds in reading the Qorân is the solicitude which Muhammed shows for the young, and especially for such as have

[1] Kerith, 2, 4.

been deprived of their natural guardians. Again and again he insists upon a kind and just treatment being accorded to children. And working upon his words, the Muhammedan doctors have framed a system of rules concerning the appointment and duties of guardians which is mos complete, and extending to the most minute details.

The great licence allowed to a man in the matter of divorce made it necessary to provide for those cases in which the wife might be with child at the time of her separation from her husband. As regards this matter the Qorân (Sûra 2, 233) ordains as follows :—

> "Mothers shall give suck to their children two full years for the father who desires the time of giving suck to be completed. And the father shall be obliged to maintain and clothe them according to what shall be reasonable. But no claim shall be made against any person beyond what he is able to meet. . . . And the same duty shall fall upon an heir. But if they (the parents) choose to wean the child (before this time) by common consent, and on mutual consideration, it shall be no crime in them. And if ye have a mind to provide a nurse for the child, it shall be no crime in you, if ye pay her what has been agreed upon, according to what is just." [1]

It will be seen from the above words that the parents have the right to arrange the matter as it may seem best to them. Under no circumstances, however, are the mother and child to be allowed to suffer.

But especially did Muhammed direct his attention to the case of orphans. His frequent references to the fatherless, and the severe punishments threatened against those who unjustly treat them and deprive them of their rights, reveal to us that better side of his character to which Muhammedan writers frequently and rightly refer.

In the distribution of a deceased man's estate, his

[1] See p. 29.

children come first in the order of inheritors. And certain instructions are given in the Qorân in order to safeguard the interests of such. Cf. Sûra 4, 4 ff. :—

> "Give not unto those who are weak of understanding [1] the substance which God hath appointed you to preserve for them; but maintain them thereout, and clothe them, and speak kindly unto them. (5) And examine the orphans until they attain the age of marriage.[2] And if ye perceive that they are able to manage their affairs well, deliver their substance unto them; and waste it not extravagantly or hastily before they grow up. (6) Let him who is rich abstain,[3] and let him who is poor take according to what shall be reasonable.[4] (7) And when ye deliver their substance unto them, bring forward witnesses thereof. But God is sufficient as reckoner."

The duties enjoined here are twofold, namely (*a*) The substance of an orphan is to be conscientiously managed, and (*b*) an appointed guardian shall take every care not to squander the estate, for which, when the time comes, he shall give full account. This is a wise and necessary law. At the handing over of the estate to the ward on his or her coming of age, the guardian is commanded to bring forward his witnesses, in order to avoid any dispute which might arise in the future. Several other passages could be quoted which show how strongly Muhammed felt upon this matter. In fact, there is nothing in the whole of the Qorân upon which he lays greater stress. Consequently, among the Muhammedans the misappropriation of the estate of an orphan is regarded as one of

[1] السُّفَهَاء, is explained in Galâlain's commentary as— والنساء والصبيان المبذّرين من الرجال, that is, extravagant men, women, and children. See also Lane, Lex.

[2] According to the Shâfïees the age is 15 years; according to the Hanafees it is 18 years. See the commentaries and law-books.

[3] That is, let him abstain from taking anything from the orphan's estate. Not being in need himself, he is to manage the estate gratuitously.

[4] That is, as payment for his services.

the *great* sins, the number of which is generally reckoned to be seven.[1] Let us take the following two or three quotations as examples.

Sûra 6, 153 :—" Meddle not with the substance of an orphan, otherwise than for the improvement thereof, until he attain maturity." [2]

Sûra 4, 2 :—" Give the orphans their substance, and render them not bad in exchange for good; and devour not their substance together with your own. Verily, that is a great sin."

Especially severe are the following words in Sûra 4, 11 :—

" They who devour the possessions of orphans unjustly shall swallow nothing but fire unto their bellies, and shall broil in raging flames."

Thus every care must be taken of children and of their possessions. Guardians must nourish and clothe them, and treat them in a friendly manner. That is, everything is to be done in order to make their lives as pleasant as possible.[3]

As we have already observed, the enactments of the Qorân have supplied the foundation for a most comprehensive law on the subject of guardians and wards. And since this law is thus based upon the express teaching of the Qorân, we find a greater agreement here between the Shiahs and Sunnis than in any other matters of law.

The first and natural guardian of the child is the father. Among the Hanafees, when the father is dead, the guardianship of his minor children devolves upon his executor. Should the father die without having appointed an executor, and his own father be still alive,

[1] See Baidawi on Sûra 4, 35. The seven " great sins " of the Muhammedans are naturally an imitation of the seven " deadly sins " of the Christian. According to the Roman Catholic Church these are, Pride, Avarice, Luxury, Envy, Anger, Accdia, Gluttony. Cf. also Prov., chap. 6.

[2] So also Sûra 17, 36.

[3] Cf. تَطِيب بها نفوسهم Baidawi on Sûra 4, 4.

the guardianship falls to him. Should the grandfather also be dead, the guardianship devolves upon his executor. Among the Shiahs, if the grandfather be alive, he is entitled to the guardianship in preference to the father's executor. In default of the natural as well as the testamentary guardians, that is, the father and his executor, and the grandfather and his executor, the obligation of appointing a guardian for the preservation and management of a minor's property rests with the judge as representing the Government.[1]

There are numerous other matters connected with the law of guardianship upon some of which the different schools are agreed, and others again concerning which there is a wide difference of opinion. But as we have to do chiefly with the teaching of the Qorân itself, we may well pass these matters by. However, we may mention that among the Hanafees if a person sufficiently qualified to undertake the guardianship of the minors can be found among the male agnates of the deceased father, such person should be appointed by the judge in preference to a stranger. But no relative, other than the father or grandfather, has any right to interfere in any way with the property of a minor unless appointed by the judge.

These enactments agree substantially with what we find in the Roman law.[2] According to this, if the deceased father had not appointed a guardian, the agnates were compelled to act as the natural guardians. If the choice of the father, and the line of consanguinity afforded no sufficient guardian, the failure was supplied by the nomination of the praetor of the city or the president of the province.

It is quite evident that the stress laid by Muhammed upon the just and humane treatment of orphans was occasioned by the injustice and violence to which widows and orphans were subjected by the Arabs of his time.

[1] See Syed Ameer Ali, "The Personal Law of the Mahommedans," p. 410 f. As regards the Shâfïees, cf. Sachau, "Muh. Recht," p. 351.

[2] See Syed Ameer Ali, "The Personal Law of the Mahommedans," Introduction, p. 3.

Before we leave this matter, we may refer briefly to some remarks of another character which are made by the prophet regarding children. As is well known, among the ancients, children, and especially male children, were generally regarded as wealth.[1] And this point of view regarding them is taken in the Qorân, where Muhammed in several passages speaks of wealth and children together.[2] Nevertheless the prophet sees in children a danger against which the believer must be on his guard, namely, the possibility that they might hinder him in the performance of his duties towards God. Cf. Sûra 63, 9 :—

"O ye believers, let not your wealth or your children direct you from the remembrance of God; for whosoever doeth this will suffer loss."

Sûra 64, 14 f. :—"O ye believers, verily in your wives and your children ye have enemies,[3] therefore beware of them. . . . (15) Your wealth and your children are only a temptation."

Sûra 18, 44 :—"Wealth and children are indeed an ornament of the earthly life; but the abiding good works are better in the sight of thy Lord, with respect to reward."

In a parable which is given in this Sûra the rich man says (verse 31) to the poor man, "I am superior to thee in wealth, and more powerful as regards people." To this the other answers (verse 32), "Although thou seest me to be inferior to thee in wealth and children, so will my Lord bestow on me a better gift than thy garden," etc.[4]

The above quotations show us, what, indeed, is insisted upon throughout the Qorân, that, with Muhammed, allegiance to God is of supreme importance. Nothing must be allowed to stand between a man and his duty to

[1] Cf. Job, chap. 1. Ps. 127, 3–5.

[2] *e.g.* Sûras 3, 8; 8, 28; 18, 44; 34, 36; 57, 19; 63, 9; 64, 15.

[3] Cf. 1 Cor. 7, 25 ff. The prophet means that wives and children can easily turn them away from their duties.

[4] See further Sûras 3, 8; 8, 28; 63, 9.

Allah. We shall return to this subject in the following section.

2. *The Duties of Children towards their Parents.*

Filial duty occupies a prominent place in the history of the ancients generally. Thus we read in the Analects of Confucius, " Filial piety and fraternal submission, are they not the root of all benevolent actions? " In this religion, filial piety is exalted above all things, and is made to include not only obedience and reverence to parents while they are living, but also sacrificial rites, full mourning and keeping to their ways when they are dead." [1] And the same is true of the ancient Egyptians. The sons were required to pay great deference to their parents, and to serve them much as in China.[2]

It is only natural, therefore, that we should expect to find much on this subject in the Qorân, especially when one also takes into consideration how much reverence is paid by children to their parents in Muhammedan countries. In fact, in almost every group of legislative revelations a place is given to the respect due to parents.

On the other hand, the prophet, consistent with his whole teaching, regards obedience and faithfulness to God of greater importance than even filial duty. We shall confine ourselves to the few following quotations :—

Sûra 29, 7 :—

" We have commanded man to show kindness towards his parents. But if they endeavour to prevail upon thee to associate with me that concerning which thou hast no knowledge, obey them not." [3]

In Sûra 31, 12 ff., we have an admonition delivered by Loqmân [4] to his son, in which he says :—

[1] Bettany, " The World's Religions," p. 115 f.
[2] *Id.*, p. 480.
[3] See also Sûras 46, 14, and 6, 152.
[4] On Loqmân, see Sale, Koran, note, p. 307 and Margoliouth, "Mohammed," p. 22.

"O my son, give not a partner unto God, for polytheism is a great impiety. (13) And we have given unto man duties towards his parents,—for his mother hath carried him (in the womb) in weakness, and for two years hath given him suck—and have said unto him, Be grateful unto me and to thy parents; unto me shall thy way be. (14) But if they endeavour to prevail on thee to associate with me that concerning which thou hast no knowledge, obey them not. Bear them company in this world in what shall be reasonable; and follow the way of him who sincerely turneth unto me."

Here Muhammed appears to be speaking under the influence of the Hebrew Decalogue. "It is not in the least surprising," says Hirschfeld,[1] "that Muhammed endeavoured to imitate the Jewish Decalogue, or rather, to adapt it to the requirements of Islâm. This fact has not only been recognized by European scholars (as Sprenger), but also by Muhammedan commentators. In his "Kitâb al-'Arâ'is," at-Ta'âlibî discusses the Decalogue, and concludes with the remark that Allah had also given it to the prophet, and quotes the two passages in the Qorân in which it is found." These passages are Sûra 17 (middle) and 6, 152–154. In the first of these we read:—

"Thy Lord hath commanded that ye worship Him only, and that ye do good unto your parents, whether the one of them, or both of them attain to old age with thee. And say not unto them 'uphi,'[2] and reproach them not, but speak kindly to them, and submit to act humbly towards them, out of tender affection, and say, 'O Lord, have

[1] "New Researches," p. 81.

[2] On the word أُفٍّ in the sentence ولا تَقُلْ لَهُمَا أُفٍّ Lane (Lex.) says, أُفّ also, is a word expressive of vexation, distress of mind, or disgust; or of dislike, displeasure, or hatred. And in our sentence here he gives it the meaning; Do not thou deem anything of their affairs burdensome, nor be contracted in bosom thereby, nor be rough, or harsh, or coarse to them . . . or do not then say to them anything expressive of the least disgust, when they have become old, but take upon thyself their service."

mercy on them both, as they nursed me when I was a child."

We see, therefore, that the greatest importance is attached in the Qorân to filial piety. In fact, disobedience to parents is reckoned among the seven grievous sins to which reference has already been made. And that such stress on this matter has not been laid in vain by the prophet may be seen from the words used by Lane in writing of the Egyptian children. He says: [1] "However much the children are caressed and fondled, in general they feel and manifest a most profound and praiseworthy respect for their parents. . . . An undutiful child is very seldom heard of among the Egyptians, or the Arabs in general." Also Prof. A. Fischer, under whom I had the privilege of studying at Leipzig, and who has spent much time in Morocco, says that while there he had repeated proofs of how sons, while yet in their boyhood, treated their mothers most brutally, but the fathers there also were treated with great respect, so that, for instance, even a grown-up son would not smoke in the presence of his father, would not sit down unbidden, etc.

The manner in which this matter is regarded by the Jewish-Christian lawgivers is so well-known that it is not necessary to deal at length with it. We have already referred to the Decalogue. Here we read, "Honour thy father and thy mother;[2] that thy days may be long upon the land, which the Lord thy God giveth thee" (Ex. 20, 12). And this, as St. Paul reminds us,[3] "is the first commandment with promise." According to Deut. 21, 18 ff. a stubborn and rebellious son was to be put to death by stoning; and with this the words of Jesus Christ in Matt. 15, 4 ff. agrees. Also in the Book of the Covenant death is prescribed as the penalty for smiting (Ex. 21, 15)

[1] "Modern Egyptians," chap. 2, p. 70.

[2] "It is not without significance that the words, 'and thy mother,' were added, seeing that, in many ancient nations, aged mothers were slain, and the mother was always subjected after her husband's death to the eldest son."—Farrar, "The Voice from Sinai," p. 187, note.

[3] Eph. 6, 1 f.; 1 Tim. 5, 4.

and also (verse 17) for cursing father or mother. With this we may compare Hammurabi where the offending son is to be punished by the loss of the member (tongue, eyes, hands) by means of which the sin was committed.[1] Finally we will refer to a passage in the Talmud, in which faithfulness towards God and obedience to parents are mentioned together :—

> " If a father saith (to his son, if he is a priest), ' defile thyself,' or, ' Make not restitution (of the thing found to its owner),' shall he obey him ? Therefore, it is written ; Let every man reverence his father and mother, but keep my Sabbaths all of you (Lev. 19, 3) ; ye are all bound to honour me." [2]

With these words, as we have seen, the teaching of Muhammed is in entire agreement. While he lays great stress upon one's duty to honour and obey his parents, still can this only be expected in what is reasonable and consonant with one's duty to God.

3. *The Law Concerning Adoption.*

It was a custom among the ancient Arabs to regard their adopted sons as being as nearly related to them as their natural sons. And so the same impediments of marriage arose from that supposed relation, in the prohibited degrees, as it would have done in the case of a natural son.[3] This custom was such as Muhammed had every reason to abolish ; and this he actually did. But it will be seen that he took this course, not in the interest of his followers, but rather in order to be able to satisfy his own lust. This disgraceful incident in the prophet's life is so well known that there is no need to dwell at

[1] §§ 192 f., 195.

[2] Jebhamoth, 6. See Geiger, " Was hat Mohammed aus dem Judenthume aufgenommen ? " p. 86.

[3] See W. R. Smith, " Kinship and Marriage," p. 52 :—" We learn that to preserve the doctrine of tribal homogeneity it was feigned that the adopted son was veritably and for all effects of the blood of his new father." Cf. also Gibbon, " Roman Empire," Vol. 3, p. 230. " The profane lawgivers of Rome . . . treated affinity and adoption as a just imitation of the ties of blood."

length upon it. Zaid b. Hârithah, adopted son of Muhammed, and one of his most zealous followers, had taken to wife Zainab bint Gahsh, whom on one occasion the prophet had seen unveiled, and whose charms had made a great impression upon him. On hearing this, Zaid at once decided to divorce her in favour of his benefactor. Muhammed, however, at first hesitated to marry one who was the divorced wife of his adopted son, a thing which, as we have seen, was prohibited by Arabic custom.[1] At length, however, the prophet received a revelation which chided his fear of man, and declared that adoption constituted no real relationship. Cf. Sûra 33, 4 f.

> " God hath given to no man two hearts within him. Neither hath he made your wives (from whom ye are wont to separate yourselves with the declaration, and regarding them afterwards as your mothers) your true mothers; nor hath he made your adopted sons your true sons.[2] This is your saying in your mouths; but God speaketh the truth, and directeth in the right way. (5) Call such as are adopted sons, the sons of their natural fathers. This is more just before God. And if ye know not their fathers,[3] let them be as your brethren in religion, and your clients."

By the words, " God hath given no man two hearts within him," is meant, that a man cannot have the same affection for supposed parents or children as for those who are really so; and, therefore, adoption should create no difficulty in the matter of marriage.

Again, in verse 37 we read :—

> " But when Zaid had determined the matter concerning her, we gave her unto thee for wife, so that no

[1] He hesitated because the marriage would be contrary to his own law (Sûra 4, 27). Cf. W. R. Smith, *id.*, and Wellhauser, " Die Ehe bei den Arabern, p. 441, Anm. 3.

[2] On دَعِيّ cf. Lane, Lex. " One who makes a claim in respect of relationship; *i.e.*, one who claims as his father a person who is not his father . . . or one who is claimed as a son by a person who is not his father; an adopted son."

[3] That is, if he be a foundling, or one taken in war.

> crime might be charged against the believers, who marry the wives of their adopted sons, when these no longer demand them. The command of God must be performed."

It will thus be seen that the only reference made by the prophet to the matter of adoption is due entirely to self-interest; the desire to set himself right with his followers in the affair regarding Zainab. There is nothing here, therefore, for which a parallel need be expected in other social legislations. For beyond abolishing the old Arabic custom already referred to, Muhammed says nothing whatever on the subject of adoption. It may be well, however, before dismissing the subject to refer briefly to the teaching of the Muslim doctors regarding the matter.

The only form of filiation which is recognized by Muhammedan law is the one which is created by *iqrâr*,—"acknowledgment." The father alone has the right to establish this relationship, to the total exclusion of the mother and all other relations. And in order to render the acknowledgment valid and effectual in law three conditions must be complied with, namely (1) The adopter and the adopted must be respectively of such ages as would admit of the possibility of their standing in the relation of parent and child to each other. A man cannot establish the relationship of father and son between himself and another unless he be at least twelve and a half years older than he whom he intends to adopt or acknowledge.[1] (2) The person to be acknowledged must be of unknown descent. If the parentage be known no ascription can take place to the acknowledger. (3) The person acknowledged must believe himself to be the adopter's son; or, at all events, if old enough, must himself assent to the act of adoption.

An infant who is too young to understand what the relationship implies, or to give an account of himself,

[1] With the Shi'ites no definite age is mentioned; one is rather to be guided by what may be regarded as the natural possibility.

is not required to agree to the acknowledgment; nor is his assent a condition precedent to the validity of an acknowledgment, as it is in the case of an adult.

It may be mentioned also that an acknowledgment produces all the legal effects of natural sonship, and vests in the child the right of inheriting from the acknowledger.

Further, in order to make an acknowledgment of a child by a married woman valid, it must be confirmed by her husband's own declaration. Other matters treated under this head by the Muslim doctors we pass by. Ample compensation has been made by them for the meagreness with which the subject is treated by Muhammed himself in the Qorân.[1]

[1] See Syed Ameer Ali, "The Personal Law of the Mahommedans," p. 166 ff. In the Hammurabi code the subject is treated in § 185 ff. No legal and complete transference of filial rights and duties seems to have existed in the law of Israel. The failure of heirs was provided for by the levirate law. See also Art. "Marriage" in Hastings' "Dictionary of the Bible."

B. LAWS CONCERNING SLAVES

Aristotle maintains that slavery is based on nature, and that certain races are intended to be subject. Whether this be true or not, it would be useless to hope for the abolition of slavery in Muhammedan countries under present conditions. Whether the prophet of Islâm could have abolished slavery altogether among his followers is very doubtful; and his prescriptions regarding the just and humane treatment of this unfortunate class, taken all in all, are praiseworthy. On the other hand, there is nothing whatever in Islâm that tends to the abolition of this curse. As Muir has well said, " Rather, while lightening, he riveted the fetter. . . . There is no obligation whatever on a Moslem to release his slaves." [1]

The matters to be treated in this section are :—

I. *The acquisition of slaves.*
II. *The treatment of slaves.*
III. *The emancipation of slaves.*

I. The Acquisition of Slaves

" The greatest of all divisions, that between freeman and slave, appears as soon as the barbaric warrior spares the life of his enemy when he has him down, and brings him home to drudge for him and till the soil." [2] The two main causes of slavery are *want* and *war*, and of these two it may be said that war is the more potent. And so with the Muhammedans, the acquisition of slaves was chiefly connected with warfare. In Sûra 47 Muhammed commands his followers thus (verse 4 f.) :—

[1] Sir W. Muir, " The Coran, its Composition and Teaching," p. 58.
[2] Tylor, " Anthropology," p. 434 ff.; also Hastings, " D.B." Vol. 4, p. 461.

"When ye encounter the unbelievers, strike off their heads, until ye have made a great slaughter among them; then bind (the remainder) in fetters. (5) And after this give (the latter) either a free dismission, or exact a ransom, until the war shall have laid down its arms." [1]

The usual expression for female slaves in the Qorân as we have already seen (p. 10) is, "that which your right hands possess." [2]

It will be seen that Muhammed says nothing in the Qorân regarding the purchase of slaves.[3]

According to Muhammedan law, a slave is (i) a person taken captive in war, or carried off by force from a foreign hostile country, and being at the time of capture an unbeliever. (ii) The child of a female slave whose father is (*a*) a slave, or, (*b*) is not the owner of the mother of the child, or (*c*) is the owner of the mother, but who does not acknowledge himself to be the father. (iii) A person acquired by purchase.

War and slavery, as one would expect, is also closely bound together in the Old Testament. In Num, chap. 31, the children of Israel are commanded to wage a war of vengeance against the Midianites. And in verse 7 ff, we read:—

[1] Cf. also Sûra 8, 12, 68. The Hanafees are of the opinion that this severe law was intended only for the Battle of Badr (A.D. 624), or has been abrogated. The Shiahs, on the other hand, regard it as always binding, and believe it to be the duty of Muhammedans to put to death all those who fall into their hands while the war is going on; but as regards those who fall into their hands later, they are to release them either free or for a ransom, or in exchange for Muhammedan prisoners, or else to keep them as slaves. (See Sale on the above passage.) The teaching of the Shâfiees is given briefly in Baidawi's commentary on the same passage.

[2] مَا مَلَكَتْ أَيْمَانُهُم (أَيْمانكم) This expression can also naturally refer to male slaves. See Sûras 4, 40; 16, 73; 24, 33, 57; 30, 27, etc.

[3] "Slavery by purchase was unknown during the reigns of the first four Caliphs. . . . There is, at least, no authentic record of any slave having been acquired by purchase during their tenure of the office. But with the accession of the usurping House of Ommiah, a change came over the spirit of Islâm. Moâwiyah was the first Mussulman sovereign who introduced into the Muhammedan world the practice of acquiring slaves by purchase." Syed Ameer Ali, "The Personal Law of the Mahommedans," Introduction, p. 38 f.

"And they warred against Midian, as the Lord commanded Moses, and they slew every male. . . . (9) And the children of Israel took captive the women of Midian and their little ones," etc.

As far as strangers were concerned, the Israelites were allowed to buy, sell, or transfer their male and female slaves. So we read in Lev. 25, 44 ff. :—

"And as for thy bondmen, and thy bondmaids, which thou shalt have; of the nations that are round about you, of them shall ye buy bondmen and bondmaids. (45) Moreover of the children of the strangers that do sojourn among you, of them shall ye buy, and of their families that are with you, which they have begotten in your land; and they shall be your possession.[1] (46) And ye shall make them an inheritance for your children after you,[2] to hold for a possession; of them shall ye take your bondmen for ever."

As among the Muhammedans slaves consist partly of children of female slaves, and partly also of those that are acquired, so in the Old Testament we have the two expressions, "he that is born in the house," and "he that is bought with money."[3] This shows us that among the Israelites as among the Muhammedans the number of slaves might be multiplied by birth. This, of course, is true of all peoples who trade in slaves; since the slaves are the "possession" of their masters, their children also belong to them.

A further agreement between the Muhammedan and

[1] אֲחֻזָּה—"Possession"; esp. of land, landed property (Gen. 17, 8, etc.); then also, as here, of persons.

[2] So also with the Babylonians, "Die Sclaven durften ohne Erlaubnis ihres Herrn nicht die Scholle verlassen und gingen bei dem Tode des Besitzers ohne weiteres in die Hände seines Erben über."—Meissner, "Beiträge zum altbabylonischen Privatrecht," p. 6. See also Meissner, "Aus d. altbabyl. Recht" ("Alter Orient," VII. I.), p. 8 f.

[3] יְלִיד בַּיִת וּמִקְנַת כֶּסֶף׃ Gen. 17, 12, etc. With יליד בית cf. the Arabic تِلاد, تالِد, تَلِيد, etc., also مُوَلَّد.

Old Testament laws consists in the limitation of slaves to foreigners. In Lev. 25, 39 ff., we read :—

> "And if thy brother be waxen poor with thee, and sell himself unto thee; thou shalt not make him to serve as a bondservant: (40) as an hired servant, and as a sojourner, he shall be with thee; he shall serve with thee unto the year of jubile: (41) then shall he go out from thee, he and his children with him . . . (42) . . . they shall not be sold as a slave is sold." [1]

And so with the Muhammedans, who are strictly forbidden to take believers as slaves. The Muhammedan like the Israelite is to regard his fellow-believer as a brother.[2]

Among the Babylonians, however, it was otherwise. Slaves were recruited both from within and without. If a son, whether natural or adopted, sinned against his parents, his father could sell him as a slave. And likewise the husband had the right to dispose of a quarrelsome wife for money. Also the captured enemy naturally took the position of a slave; especially did the white (light-complexioned) slaves from Gutium and Shubarti at that time appear to be much desired.[3]

II. The Treatment of Slaves

We have already seen how the prophet in the Qorân insists upon the just and humane treatment of the widow and orphan. And a like treatment is demanded by him also for slaves; and that in accordance with his teaching that all men belong to God, and are therefore in a certain sense alike. So we read in Sûra 16, 73 :—

> "God hath caused some to excel others in worldly possessions; yet those who thus excel do not give

[1] This law, however, can only be regarded as an ideal. That Israelites could be taken as slaves, and, in fact, were often so taken, usually on account of debt, we find from such passages as 2 Kings, 4, 1; Ex. 21, 2 ff.; Deut. 15, 12; Jer. 34, 9 ff.; Isa. 50, 1.

[2] See Syed Ameer Ali, "The Personal Law of the Mahommedans," p. 37 f.

[3] Meissner, "Beiträge zum altbabylonischen Privatrecht," p. 6.

of their wealth unto those whom their right hands possess (their slaves), so that both may have an equal share thereof. Do they, therefore, deny the beneficence of God?"

Also Sûra 4, 40:—

"Honour God, and associate none with him; and show kindness unto parents, relations, orphans, the poor, the neighbour who is of kin to you, and he who is not,[1] and to your trusted friend, and the traveller, and to those whom your right hands possess; for God loveth not the arrogant and the proud."

In the year before his death, the prophet, during a farewell pilgrimage at Minâ, delivered an address to his followers, in which, among several other injunctions, we find the following:—

"And your slaves! see that ye feed them with such food as ye eat yourselves, and clothe them with the like clothing as ye wear yourselves; and if they commit a fault which ye are inclined not to forgive, sell them; for they are the servants of the Lord, and are not to be tormented."[2]

If Muhammed could not abolish slavery, he has certainly done what he could to secure for slaves a humane treatment. And if present-day Muhammedans disregard his injunctions, it is not fair to hold the prophet himself responsible for it.[3] Also, as already observed, it must not

[1] الجَارُ الجُنُبُ "The person who is one's neighbour, but who belongs to another people."—Lane, Lex.

[2] Muir, "Life of Mahomet," Vol. I (London), p. 486.

[3] Prof. Fischer says, "Dass man sich die Lage der Sklaven in heutigen muslimischen Ländern im allgemeinen nicht zu schlimm vorstellen darf, hat, abgeschen von andern (s. z. B. Lane, "Modern Egyptians," p. 168), besonders Snouck Hurgronje gezeigt ("Mekka," 2, p. 18 ff). Bei meinem zweimaligen Aufenthalte in Marokko habe ich gleichfalls den Eindruck jewonnen, dass die Lage der Muslimischen Sklaven nur formell von der christlicher Diener verschieden ist." Cf. also Doughty, "Arabia Deserta," I, p. 554.—"The condition of the slave is always tolerable and is often happy in Arabia; bred up as poor brothers of the sons of the household, they are a manner of God's wards of the pious Mohammedan householder who is *ammy* [properly 'my uncle'] of their servitude and *abûy* ['my father']. . . . It is not many years 'if their

be forgotten that the legislation of the Qorân was enacted for a seventh-century people. The position and treatment of slaves among the ancients in different lands naturally differed in accordance with the character of the various peoples, as well as the character of the slaves themselves, that is, *e.g.*, whether they be foreign or home-born. And there was also a difference of treatment by the same peoples at different times.[1] But if the enactments of the prophet were only faithfully observed by his followers, the treatment of slaves in Muhammedan countries would in all cases compare very favourably with what it was among the ancients.

Also the treatment of slaves, as enacted in Muhammedan law, taken all in all, can only be regarded as just. As we have already seen in the case of adultery (p. 39), female slaves were held to be less guilty than free women, and consequently their punishment was to be less severe.

---

houselord fears Allah' before he will give them their liberty; and then he sends them not away empty; but in upland Arabia (where only substantial persons are slave-holders) the good man will marry out his free servants, male and female, endowing them with somewhat of his own substance, whether camels or palmstems."

[1] As regards the Babylonians cf. Meissner, "Beitr. z. altbab. Privatrecht," p. 6 f.,—"Der Sclave war nach altbabylonischem Rechte kein Mensch, sondern eine Sache, welche man stückweise berechnete; deshalb wird von ihm immer als 1, SAG *ardu* = 1 Stuck (eigentlich Kopf = caput) geredet, und aus eben dem Grunde wird auch nie der Name seines Vaters genannt. Von den Freien waren sie Schon äusserlich durch ein eingebranntes Mal unterschieden, häubig, und besonders wohl, wenn sie als Ausreisser bekannt waren, trugen sie sogar Ketten. . . . Auch die Todesstrafe konnte natürlich ohne weiteres gegen sie angewandt werden. . . . Trotzdem die Sclaven ihrem Herrn absolut rechtlos gegenüberstanden, wird das Verhältnis zwischen Herrn und Diener gewöhnlich ein recht freundliches gewesen sein. Die Sclavin war gewöhnlich die Nebenfran ihres Gebieters . . . der ihre Kinder zu erziehen verpflichtet war. . . . In gleicher Weise wird auch der Sclave gut behandelt worden sein; ja es kam sogar vor, dass Sclaven adoptiert wurden. . . . Ein anderer Weg, die Freiheit zu erlangen, war der Loskauf durch Geld (ipṭiru)."

Also as regards the Israelites, cf. Guthe, "Bibelwörterbuch," art. "Sklaven," "Der älteste Haussklave . . . hatte eine sehr angesehene Stellung und unter Urnständen Erbrecht (Gen. 15, 2 f.]. Eine Sklavin konnte durch den Herrn zur Gattin und Gebieterin des Hauses erhoben werden. Man gab den Sklaven Weiber aus den eigenen Töchtern 1, Chron. 2, 35 und den Sklavinnen eigene Söhne zu Männern, Ex. 21, 9. . . . Die grausame Behandlung von Sklaven, auf die Luc. 12, 46 ff. anspielt, ist römisch oder herodeisch, nicht israelitisch."

And especially did the law enact that they should be sufficiently supported, and not made to suffer.

On the other hand, it must be remembered that slaves, like any other property, were transferable. A Muhammedan has the right to sell his concubine, at least as long as he has no child by her.[1] And even if he have a child by her, he can always deny the paternity (although this does not often happen). And in any case, the slave would have to continue to serve him, and be his concubine, that is unless he, when she has borne a son to him, presents her with her freedom by way of compensation.

III. The Emancipation of Slaves

The founder of Islâm not only insisted upon the humane treatment of slaves, but also that it should be made possible for them to secure their freedom, when they had shown themselves worthy of it by their conduct. Accordingly the emancipation of slaves among the Muhammedans must be regarded as a meritorious act.[2] Sûra 24, 33 reads :—

> " And those of your slaves who desire a deed of manumission,[3] write [4] it for them, if ye have a good

[1] Cf. Hammurabi § 119.—" If a debt has seized a man, and he has handed over for the money a maidservant who has borne him children, the money the merchant paid to him the owner of the maid shall pay (back), and he shall ransom his maid."

[2] Cf. Sachau, " Muh. Recht," p. 131.

[3] الكتاب cf. Lane, Lex., under كَاتَبَهُ—" He (a slave) made a written (or other) contract with him (his master), that he (the former) should pay a certain sum as the price of himself, and on the payment thereof be free . . . also he (a master) made such a contract with him (his slave). . . . The slave in this case is called مُكَاتَب . . . and also مُكَاتِب and so is the master; the act being mutual. . . . But the lawyers in the present day call the slave مُكَاتَب only; and the master, مُكَاتِب."

[4] On this imper. cf. Baidawi on the passage—الأَمْر فيه للنَّدْب عند أكثر العلماء لأنّ الكتابة معاوَضة تتضمّن الارناق فلا تجب كغيرها Thus we see that according to the majority of the jurists it has the meaning only of exhortation, since it has to do with a contract which enjoins duties and rights on both parties.

opinion of them, and give them of the wealth of God, which he has given you."

The manner in which this emancipation is brought about in Muhammedan countries varies. Sometimes complete and immediate emancipation is granted to a slave gratuitously, or for a money compensation to be paid later. This is done by means of a written document, or by a verbal declaration in the presence of two witnesses: or again by the master presenting the slave with the certificate of sale obtained from the former master. Also, in conformity with the prophet's demand in Sûra 24, 33, future emancipation is sometimes agreed upon to be granted on the fulfilment of certain conditions; or more frequently, upon the death of the owner. In the latter case the owner cannot sell the slave with whom the agreement has been made.[1] Also, as the owner cannot alienate by will more than one-third of the whole property that he leaves, the law ordains that, if the value of the said slave exceed that portion, the slave must obtain, and pay to the owner's heirs the additional sum. We shall see further on that for certain offences, such as manslaughter, etc., the freeing of a captive is reckoned as part-punishment.[2]

It is not impossible that Muhammed to some extent, at any rate, was acquainted with the Old Testament enactments concerning the emancipation of slaves (cf. Deut. 15, 12; Ex. 21, 2 ff.; Jer. 34, 15, 17; Ezek. 46, 17). While, however, the Old Testament deals only with the emancipation of Israelite slaves, who had become bondmen through debt, Muhammed speaks of the emancipation of all slaves.

[1] See Lane, "Modern Egyptians," p. 115 f.; also Sachau, "Muh. Recht," p. 131 ff.

[2] See also Margoliouth, "Mohammed," p. 461 f.

C. LAWS CONCERNING INHERITANCE

Before we proceed to deal with the question of the distribution of an estate, a few words must be said concerning :—

I. THE WILL

While providing for the attestation of witnesses, Muhammed's chief concern was to prevent the possibility of false swearing in the matter. And so in Sûra 5, 105 ff., he enacts that the will of a deceased person shall be attested by trustworthy witnesses. He says :—

" O ye believers, let there be testimony among you, when any one of you is near death, at the time of making the will, through two just men from amongst you,[1] or two others from a different people,[2] if ye be on a journey, and the calamity of death befall you, ye shall shut them both up after the prayer;[3] then, if ye doubt them, they shall swear by God (and say), ' We will not sell our testimony for a price, even though it were to a relative, neither will we conceal God's testimony. Verily, should we then be amongst sinners.' (106) But if it shall be made clear that both of these have been guilty of sin, then let two others stand up in their place, of those who think them to be guilty, the two nearest in kin; and they shall both swear by God, ' Verily, our testimony is truer

[1] That is, from among the believers.

[2] Those scholars who regard the words آخَرَانِ مِنْ غَيْرِكُمْ as referring to non-Moslims in Moslim countries (أهل الذمّة) hold that the enactment is abrogated, since the testimony of a non-Moslim against a Moslim is universally agreed to be inadmissable (see Baidawi on the passage). Abû Hanîfa and Ibn Hanbal, however, would allow the testimony of a non-Moslim under certain circumstances. See Sachau, " Muh. Recht," p. 739.

[3] Usually the midday prayer is meant, this being the chief prayer.

than the testimony of those two, and we have not transgressed. For then we should surely be of the unjust.' (107) Thus it is easier for men to bear testimony according to the purport thereof; else must they fear lest an oath be given to rebut their own oath. Therefore fear God, and hearken; for God guideth not the people who do ill."

Thus we see that two witnesses at least are necessary in order to render a will valid.[1] And it is clear also that the prophet (at least at first) would allow as witnesses men who did not belong to the Muhammedan religion. These witnesses are to be shut up "after the prayer," so as to prevent any influence from being brought to bear upon them.[2]

II. The Distribution of the Inheritance

The enactments of the Qorân concerning the distribution of a deceased person's estate are, on the whole, equitable, and show a great advance upon the unjust, and indeed cruel customs which obtained among the Arabs in pre-Islamic times. The chief object kept in view by the pagan Arabs in the succession of the property was that of retaining it in the family. And in order to secure this object the right to succeed was confined exclusively to the male relations, and even among them to those who were capable of bearing arms, and of defending their possessions.[3] Consequently, all female relations as well as all male minors were excluded from the right to succeed. The widows were excluded because they were regarded as

[1] But see further the commentaries and law-books.

[2] We may give here another passage, the first part of which is held to be abrogated, namely Sûra 2, 176 ff.:—"It is prescribed for you that when one of you is face to face with death, if ye leave any goods, the legacy is to his parents, and to his kinsmen, according to what is reasonable, as a duty on those who fear God. (177) And if one shall alter the legacy after that he has heard it, the sin thereof is only upon those who alter it. Verily, God heareth and knoweth (all things). (178) And he who fears from the testator an injustice (unintentional) or a crime, and shall make a settlement between the parties, it is no sin to him."

[3] على سُنّة الجاهليّة فإنّهم ما كانوا يورثون النساءَ والأطفال ويقولون إنّما يرث من يحارِب ويذُبّ عن الحَوْزة Baidawi on Sûra 4, 8. See also W. Rob. Smith, "Kinship and Marriage," p. 65 ff.

part of the estate, and as such passed ordinarily into the hands of their husband's heirs; the daughters were excluded because upon their marriage they ceased to be members of their natural families; finally, the male minors were excluded because as yet they were not able to bear arms, and so to defend the tribal property, rights, and privileges. These unjust customs the prophet boldly undertook to abolish; and so to help the female sex and the children to secure their just rights.

At first, however, in Medina Muhammed had a design as regards succession which is totally different from that which we find in his later enactments. It is set forth that all natural relationships shall be disregarded in favour of a spiritual or religious relationship, and that the succession was to be regulated accordingly. Thus we read in Sûra 8, 73:—

> "Verily, those who believe and have fled (from Mecca), and with their wealth and persons have fought for the cause of God, and those who have given refuge (to the prophet and his Meccan followers) and help, these shall consider themselves as next of kin to each other. But those who do believe, but have not fled, ye have nought to do with their claims of kindred, until they flee as well. But if they ask you for aid for the sake of religion, then help is due from you, except against a people between whom and you there is an alliance."

Thus we see that those of the believers who had fled with the prophet out of Mecca, the Muhâgirûn, were to regard the Medinan believers, the Ansârs, as their nearest relations, and consequently these were to inherit from each other, to the exclusion of blood-relations. It is clear that this enactment prevailed for a long time, as we gather from Baidawi.[1] Eventually, however, it was held to be abrogated through the last words in the same Sûra:—

[1] كان المهاجرون والأنصار يتوارثون بالهِجْرة والنُصْرة دون الأقارب حتّى نُسِخَ بقوله وَأُولُوا الأَرْحامِ بَعْضُهم أَوْلَى بِبَعْضٍ أو بالنصرة والمظاهة Baidawi on Sûra 8, 73.

> " But blood-relations are nearer in kin by the Book of God."

And similar words are found also in Sûra 33, 6 :—

> " Blood-relations are nearer in kin to each other by the Book of God than the believers and those who fled."

Important as regards the questions of succession and the division of the estate are the directions given in Sûra 4, 12 ff. :—

> " God commands you concerning your children. For a male the like of the portion of two females. But if there be females only, and above two in number, they shall have two-thirds of what the deceased leaves. If there be but one, then let her have a half. The parents of the deceased shall have, each of them, a sixth part of what he leaves, if he has a child; but if he leave no child, and his parents alone be his heirs, then let his mother have a third.[1] And if he have brethren, let his mother have a sixth,[2] after payment of the bequests he has made, and of his debts. . . . (13) And ye shall have half of what your wives leave, if they die without issue; but if they leave children, then ye shall have a fourth of what they leave, after payment of bequests made, and of their debts. (14) The wives shall have a fourth of what ye leave, if ye die without issue. But if ye leave children, then let them have an eighth of what ye leave, after payment of bequests made, and of debts. (15) If a man or a woman's property be inherited by a distant relative (neither son nor father),[3] and he have a brother or sister, then let each of these two have a sixth; but if there be more brothers or sisters, let them share in a third, after payment of the bequest he bequeaths, and of his debts."

[1] The remaining two-thirds shall go to the father according to the first enactment in this verse.

[2] What remains goes naturally to the father.

[3] كَلَالَة denotes " remote relationship " [Cognatio haud proscima. Arabes dicunt " هو ابن عم الكلالة vel ابن عم كلالة Ille cognatus paulum remotus est.—Freytag]. See also Baidawi on the verse.

Again, at the end of the same Sûra we read :—

> " They will ask thee for a decision. Say, God will give you a decision concerning remote kinship. If a man die, and have no child, but have a sister, let her have half of what he leaves. And he (the brother) shall be her heir, if she have no issue. But if there be two sisters, let them both have two-thirds of what he leaves. And if there be more brothers and sisters, let the male have like the portion of two females."

It must be admitted that these laws concerning inheritance, in spite of the fact that they were promulgated with the best intention, and in spite of the fact also that they appear on first sight most minute and definite, yet are but little adapted as a basis for the formation of a complete and proper succession-law.[1] And in order to present such a law the jurists of Islâm have needed great acuteness and power of reflection. And to attempt to follow these jurists in their treatment of the different enactments would take us far beyond the limits set to our treatise. We will rather confine ourselves to those enactments which are given in the Qorân itself, as well as a few of the most important points dealt with in Muhammedan law, and shall then conclude with a few general remarks upon the same.

And first of all we notice that no privileges whatever are given to the first-born in the matter of succession. In this, however, the law of the Qorân is not without a parallel.[2] On the other hand, it will be seen that it differs

[1] See Sachau, " Muh. Recht," p. 197 ff :—" Das Verkehrte daran ist, dass sie nicht von den nächsten und natürlichsten Erben, also in ersten Linie dem Sohn, ausgehen, sondern von den Erben zweiten oder dritten Grades, denen bestimmte Quoten der Erbschaft zugewiesen werden. Indem der Qorân diese Quoten (nach denen die betr. Erben bei den juristen ذوو الفروض. ' Quoten Erben' heissen, im Gegensatze zu den عصبات, den 'allgemeinen Erben') ein für allermal festlegte, die übrigen Verwandten aber zu Resterben stempelte, wurden letztere in den Hintergrund gedrängt, so dass es vorkommen kann, dass sie Quotenerben alles erhalten und beispielsweise der natürlichste Erbe, der Sohn, nichts."

[2] Cf. the Roman Law.

entirely on this point from the Old Testament,[1] with which on so many other matters it is in entire agreement.

Another point to be noticed is, that in most cases the share of a female is equal to only half that of a male. Although one would wish that the prophet had advanced yet further in his concessions to the female sex, still it must be acknowledged that the enactments already referred to are a vast improvement upon the inhuman customs of pre-Muhammedan times. It will also be seen that where a deceased man's parents, brothers, and sisters are entitled to only a small share of the inheritance, that share is to be equal to all without distinction of sex.

Again, according to the law there is no difference as regards ability to succeed between the child of a lawful wife and that of a concubine, provided always the child of such concubine is acknowledged by her master; both inherit in like manner. And the same is the case with the child of a lawful wife, on the one hand, and an adopted child, on the other. But it is enacted that an illegitimate child shall inherit only from its mother, and vice versa. Where there is no legal heir or legatee, the property goes to the government treasury.[2]

Also, according to the law, the apostate, the Christian, the Jew (also magician), the murderer, or manslayer, and the slave are debarred from inheriting. A non-Moslim cannot inherit the property of a Moslim, even when he is his nearest relative. On this point the Sunnites and Shi'ites are agreed. With the latter, if a Moslim should die leaving only non-Moslim relations, the property goes to the Imâm, to the exclusion of such non-Moslim heirs. Among the Sunnites it goes to the government treasury. Further, among the Shi'ites a Muhammedan heir of a non-Muhammedan relative comes before a non-Muhammedan relative, even when the latter is nearer in degree

[1] See Gen. 24, 36; 25, 5; Deut. 21, 15–17; also Luke 15, 31. "The present law (*i.e.*, Deut. 21, 15–17) does not institute the right of the first-born, but invests with its sanction an established usage, and guards it against arbitrary curtailment."—Driver, "Comm," p. 247.

[2] See Lane, "Modern Egyptians," p. 118.

of relationship than the former.[1] But should a non-Moslim leave only non-Moslim relatives, the inheritance should go to them in preference to the Imâm.

In the case of a murderer, according to the Shi'ite law, the absence of an intention to kill must be clearly proved before he can succeed to the inheritance of his victim. With the Hanafees,[2] however, murder, whether intentional or unintentional, prevents one from inheriting, under any circumstances whatsoever; but, of course, the murderer must be an adult, and in full possession of his mental faculties.

Lastly, according to both the Sunnites and the Shi'ites slavery is a bar to succession. According to the latter, should a person die leaving only a slave relative, his property is to be sold, and the proceeds applied to the emancipation of the said slave. But according to the Sunnites the inheritance shall go to the Treasury. On this point the teaching of the Shi'ites is much more reasonable and just than that of the Sunnites. If a person die leaving two heirs, one a free person, and the other a slave, the whole inheritance goes to the one that is free, to the exclusion of the slave, though he (the slave) be nearer in relationship to the deceased.[3]

It will be seen that the inheritance-law of the Qorân corresponds with that of the Old Testament in one important respect, namely, in the order in which the relatives of a deceased person are to benefit. In the Old Testament this is found both in Deut. (21, 15–17), and in P. (Num. 27, 8–11). That is, a man's children come first in the order of succession, and then his nearest relatives. So we read in Num. 27, 8 ff :—

> "If a man die, and have no son, then ye shall cause his inheritance to pass unto his daughter. (9)

[1] According to some of the Shi'ite lawyers no Moslim can inherit the property of a non-Moslim. See Sachau, "Muh. Recht," p. 206.

[2] Also with the Shâfiees. See Sachau, *id.* p. 205.

[3] See Syed Ameer Ali, "The Personal Law of the Mahommedans," p. 95 ff.

> And if he have no daughter, then ye shall give his inheritance unto his brethren. (10) And if he have no brethren, then ye shall give his inheritance unto his father's brethren. (11) And if his father have no brethren, then ye shall give his inheritance unto his kinsman that is next to him of his family, and he shall possess it; and it shall be unto the children of Israel a statute of judgement, as the Lord commanded Moses."

On the other hand, as we have already seen, the Muhammedan law gives no privileges to primogeniture. And in this it differs from the Israelitic law.[1] It agrees, however, with the Babylonian law, according to which all the children, natural and adopted, inherited, only that the *primogenitus* (aḫû rabû) appears to have occupied a pre-eminent position, and to have received a larger share of the inheritance than his brethren. The remainder of the father's property, gold, slaves, real estate, etc. to be then equally divided.[2]

The Muhammedan law agrees also in this with the Roman law, where, as Gibbon says,[3] "the insolent prerogative of primogeniture was unknown; the two sexes were placed on a just level; all the sons and daughters were entitled to an equal portion of the patrimonial estate; and if any of the sons had been intercepted by a premature death, his person was represented, and his share was divided, by his surviving children."

An important agreement is found between the code of Hammurabi and the Muhammedan law concerning

[1] See Art. "Heir" in Hastings' "D. B." Vol. 2, p. 341 f.

[2] Meissner, "Beiträge zum altbabylonischen Privatrecht," p. 16. It is not clear, however, how Hammurabi, § 165, is to be taken. "If a man has apportioned to his son, whom he has favoured—sha i-in-shu maḫ-ru—field, garden, and house, has written him a sealed deed, after the father has gone to his fate, when the brothers divide, the present his father gave him he shall take, and over and above he shall share equally in the goods of the father's house." The question here is whether the expression "sha i-in-shu maḫ-ru" refers to a younger son favoured by his father, or equally, as D. H. Müller ("Die Gesetze Ḥammurabi's," p. 134 f.) maintains, to the first-born.

[3] "Roman Empire," Vol. 3, p. 234.

the right of succession of the children of a concubine. As we have already seen, no distinction is made by the Muhammedan law between the child of a legal wife and that borne by a female slave, or concubine, provided the master acknowledge the child to be his; both inherit equally. And so we read in Hammurabi, § 170:—

> "If a man his wife has borne him sons, and his maidservant has borne him sons, the father in his lifetime has said to the sons which the maidservant has borne him 'my sons,' has numbered them with the sons of his wife, after the father has gone to his fate, the sons of the wife and the sons of the maidservant shall share equally in the goods of the father's house; the sons that are sons of the wife at the sharing shall fix and take.[1]

On the other hand, if the man does not acknowledge the children of his concubine as his, they shall not inherit, according to both laws.

[1] "Er teilt und wählt sich seinem Anteil"—Winckler.

D. LAWS CONCERNING CHARITY

There is no duty to which more frequent reference is made in the Qorân than that of almsgiving. In almost every Sûra is this duty urged upon the believers; and in some Sûras, indeed, the prophet returns again and again to this subject.[1] Further, we notice that the duty of almsgiving is usually coupled with that of prayer, upon which also Muhammed lays great stress.

Alms are said to be of two kinds, namely, legal and voluntary. The word usually employed to denote the former of these two is زَكَوة or زَكَاة zakât; and for the latter—the voluntary alms صَدَقَة sadaqat. This distinction, however, is not always observed.

To the verb زكا or زَكِى two meanings are given: (*a*) to increase or augment; to receive an increase and a blessing from God; to thrive by the blessing of God; (*b*) to be, or to become pure. As to which of these two is the primary meaning there is a difference of opinion among scholars.[2] Baidawi says that these alms are called zakât either because they increase a man's store, by drawing down a blessing thereon, and produce in his soul the virtue of liberality; or because they purify the remaining part of one's substance from pollution, and the soul from the filth of avarice.

Again, the verb صَدَق means, in the first form "to speak the truth," and in the fifth form "to give alms to one," تَصَدَّقَ عَلَيْهِ, or to give what is termed صَدَقَة.

[1] See esp. Sûra 9.

[2] Heb. זכה Aram. דכא . ܙܟܐ Assyr. zakû, to be pure. Cf. Ges. H.W.B. Del. Assyr. H.W.B.

Also the verb is used to denote what is given for the sake of God; or what is given with the desire of obtaining a recompense from God. It is what one gives from one's property as a propitiation, to obtain the favour of God, and is supererogatory. The zakât, on the other hand, is obligatory.[1]

As we have observed, the references to this subject in the Qorân are exceedingly numerous; and it is clearly impossible within the limits of this work to give here even a tenth of them. The following, however, are a few of the most important.

Sûra 9, 5:—" . . . But if they repent,[2] and are steadfast in prayer, and give alms, then let them go their way. God is forgiving and merciful."

Id., 18:—" He only shall repair to the temples of God who believes in God and the last day, and is steadfast in prayer, and gives the alms, and fears only God. For these are among the rightly guided."

Id., 60:—" Alms are only for the poor and needy,[3] and those who work for them,[4] and those whose hearts are reconciled,[5] and for ransoming (captives), and for debtors (who cannot pay), and for the advancement of God's religion, and for the wayfarer."

Id., 104:—" Take from their wealth alms to cleanse and to purify them thereby; and pray for them."

Sûra 2, 269 f.:—" O ye believers, give in alms of the good things that ye have earned, and of what we have brought forth for you out of the earth; but do not take the vile thereof to spend in alms, what you would not take yourselves save by connivance." [6]

[1] See Lane, Lex. Also Ges. H.W.B. under צדקה.

[2] That is, the idolators.

[3] As to the difference in meaning between لِلْفُقَرَآءِ والمَسَاكِين, see Lane, Lex, under مِسْكِين.

[4] Namely, those who collect and distribute the same.

[5] To Islâm.

[6] Cf. Malachi, chap. 1, 8.

Sûra 3, 86 :—" Ye cannot attain to righteousness until ye expend in alms of what ye love. But what ye expend in alms, that God knoweth."

Sûra 6, 142 :—" . . . Eat from the fruit thereof whenever it bears fruit, and bring the dues thereof on the day of harvest." [1]

Sûra 41, 5 ff. :—" . . . Woe to the idolators, who give not alms, and believe not in the life to come. But as to those who believe and do right, for them is a reward that cannot be measured."

Sûra 57, 7 :—" Believe in God and His apostle, and give alms of what He has made you inheritors of. For those amongst you who believe and give alms,—for them is a great reward."

In the early days of Islâm, the obligatory alms was collected by officials especially appointed for the purpose, and applied to different causes, such as the building of mosques, the maintaining of those who served in the wars, etc. But in course of time this practice was discontinued, and it was left to the Muhammedan's conscience to give the zakât, to be applied in whatever manner he thought proper.

According to Muhammedan law, alms are to be given from five different things, namely, cattle, money, corn, fruit, and wares sold. Alms shall be given once in every year, generally in the proportion of one part in forty, or two and a half per cent. of the value of what one possesses. For every five camels, an ewe shall be given; for twenty-five camels, a pregnant camel. He who has money to the amount of two hundred dirhems of silver, or twenty mitkals (that is, thirty dirhems) of gold, must give annually the fortieth part thereof, or the value of that part.

Alms are not due for cattle employed in tilling the ground, or in the carrying of burdens. It is said in a tradition لا صَدَقَةَ فِي ٱلْإِبِلِ ٱلْجَارَّةِ—There is no ṣadaqat in the case of working-camels; because they are the riding-

[1] That is, of the fruit-trees previously referred to.

camels of the people; for the ṣadaqat is in the case of pasturing camels, and not when they work.[1]

On the other hand, in certain cases a much larger portion is stipulated than the above mentioned; that is, of what is taken out of mines, or the sea, or by any art or profession, over and above what is sufficient for the reasonable support of a man's family, and, especially, where there is a mixture, or a suspicion of unjust gain. In such cases a fifth part ought to be given in alms.[2]

It is to be noticed further that before a Muhammedan is required to give legal alms, it is necessary not only that his property shall be of a certain amount in value, but also that it shall have been in his possession for at least eleven months.

We will next consider what is said in the Qorân with regard to spoils of war. Sûra 8, entitled "The Spoils," begins thus :—

> "They will question thee about the spoils. Answer: The spoils are God's and the apostle's. Therefore, fear God, and settle this amongst yourselves."
>
> Also 42 reads :—" Know ye that when ye have taken any booty, a fifth part thereof belongeth to God and to his apostle, and to kindred, and to orphans, and to the poor, and to the wayfarer."

Thus four-fifths of what is taken in war is to be divided among those that take part in it, and the remaining one-fifth is then to be divided as above. As to the manner in which the dividing is to take place, and the particular persons who are to benefit, there is much difference of opinion among Muhammedan scholars.[3]

Words to the same effect are found also in Sûra 59, 8 :—

> "The spoils taken from the people of the towns, and assigned by God to his apostle, belongeth to God,

[1] Cf. لَيْسَ فِي ٱلرَّقِيقِ صَدَقَةٌ—"There is no ṣadaqat for slaves in cases where they are employed in service" (that is, as distinguished from slaves kept only for selling).

[2] See Sale, Prel. Dis., § 4.

[3] See Sale's Prel. Dis., § 6.

> and to the apostle, and to his kindred, and to the orphan, and to the poor, and to the wayfarer, that none of it may circulate among such only of you as are rich."

Finally we have the زكاة الفطر—The alms of the breaking of the fast. This was to be given at the end of Ramadân, the ninth of the Arabian months. It was enacted that the believers should fast during the whole of this month from dawn, when there is light enough to distinguish between a white and black thread, till sunset.[1] This alms is obligatory upon every person of the Muhammedans, the free and the slave, male and female, young and old, rich and poor. It is said to purify the faster from unprofitable and lewd discourse, and consists of a صاع [2] of dates or barley (or of raisins or some other ordinary kind of food), or half a صاع of wheat.

That the greatest value is attached to the practice of almsgiving is shown, not only by the prominence given to the matter in the Qorân itself, but also by the frequent references to the same which one meets with in tradition. Thus we read, "Give ye something as alms, though it be but a dried date; for it will supply somewhat of the want of the hungry." And again, "Give ye alms, though it be but the half of a dried date." Reference is often made by writers on the subject to a saying of the Caliph 'Omar ibn Abd-'Alzîz, namely, "Prayer carries us half-way to God; fasting brings us to the door of his palace; and alms procures for us admission." It is also related how Hasân, the son of 'Ali, and grandson of the prophet, thrice in his life-time divided his substance equally between himself and the poor, and twice gave

[1] See Sûra 2, 181 ff.

[2] صاع is a certain measure used for measuring corn, etc., upon which depend the decisions of the Muhammedans relating to measures of capacity. Mensura aridorum quatuor modios (مدّ) continens; quorum unus unam libram et tertiam eius partem pondere aequat.—Freytag, Lex.

away all he possessed. And even if we cannot believe all that is said on this matter, yet it shows us in what light almsgiving was, and is still regarded among the Muhammedans.

The hospitality of the Arabs is proverbial. Generosity stands forth as one of the noblest traits in their character. Hence the enactments of the Qorân concerning almsgiving would appeal to the Arab in an especial manner.[1]

Moreover, the enactments of the prophet are only an extension of a practice which already existed among the ancient Arabs. According to Pliny,[2] the Arabian merchants who traded in spices were not allowed to sell any until they had paid the tithe thereof to their God Sabis. And the same practice obtained among the Greeks and Romans, and, in fact, among heathen nations generally from the earliest times.

Although it may not be correct to speak of the Muhammedan alms as tithe, yet the principle in both is one and the same, especially as regards the legal alms, which, as we have seen, were originally collected by officials appointed for the purpose.[3]

Further, in laying stress upon this duty, the founder of Islâm undoubtedly had in his mind the injunctions of the Jewish and Christian codes. For in both the Old and New Testaments, as well as in the Talmudic writings, frequent references are made to the matter of almsgiving. We give the following from the Old Testament :—

Lev. 19, 9 f. :—" And when ye reap the harvest of your land, thou shalt not wholly reap the corners of thy

[1] See the Introduction.
[2] Laert. Lib. 1.
[3] " When the Arabs hastened to accept Islam they were apt to overlook one portion of its requirements, viz., the regular payment of a tax, called by a euphemism Alms. The stages by which the Alms had reached the character of a tax cannot now be traced; it began without doubt in voluntary contributions which the wealthier members of the community were desired to provide for the support of the poorer members; and indeed the names for the institution seem quite certainly Jewish terms, of which one signifies " righteousness," and the other " merit," but of which the former even in Biblical times had a tendency to signify almsgiving," etc. Margoliouth, " Mohammed," p. 412 ff.

field, neither shalt thou gather the gleanings of thy harvest. (10) And thou shalt not glean thy vineyard, neither shalt thou gather the fallen fruit of thy vineyard; thou shalt leave them for the poor, and for the stranger; I am the Lord your God."

Deut. 14, 28 f. :—" At the end of every three years thou shalt bring forth all the tithe of thine increase in the same year, and shalt lay it up within thy gates: (29) and the Levite, because he hath no portion nor inheritance with thee, and the stranger, and the fatherless, and the widow, which are within thy gates, shall come, and shall eat and be satisfied; that the Lord thy God may bless thee in all the work of thine hand which thou doest."

It is also clear that Muhammed was acquainted with the teaching of the Talmud as regards almsgiving. In the Talmud the greatest stress is laid upon this duty. Here, as in the Qorân, it is again and again referred to. The following passages may be taken as examples :—

P. Abôth 5. " There are four kinds of almsgivers, namely, those who are willing to give, but are not willing that others should give; whose eyes are envious of the goods of others. He who wishes that others give, but that he himself should not give; whose eyes are envious of his own goods. He who gives himself and also allows others to give; he is pious. He who will neither give himself, nor yet allow others to give; he is wicked."

Snh. 49 b. " Alms is more meritorious than all sacrifices."

B. Bathra. 10 b. " So great is almsgiving that it reaches even to redemption."

" As the sin-offering of Israel made expiation, so doth alms make expiation for the people."

Ber. 6 b. " Three things destroy evil fate, namely, prayer, alms, and repentance."

" What are meritorious with fasting are the alms which a man gives in the evening to the poor, that they may procure provisions."

Noteworthy also are the following sayings in the Talmud:—

"Alms is the salt of wealth. When wealth is salted with this, it keepeth, just as meat is kept from destruction with salt." [1]

"The giving of alms in secret is greater, according to the teaching of Moses."

It is said of Rabbi Janay, that seeing a man bestowing alms in a public place he said, "Thou hadst better not have given at all, than to have bestowed alms so openly, and put the poor man to shame." And Rabbi Jochanan taught that he who is active in kindnesses towards his fellows is forgiven his sin.

Muhammed also believed in the value of giving alms in secret. He says, Sûra 2, 273 :—

"If ye give your alms openly, it is well; but if ye conceal them, and give them up to the poor, this will be better for you, and will atone for your sins." [2]

And with these words regarding secrecy in almsgiving we may compare the words of Christ in Matt. 6, 1 :—

"Take heed that ye do not your alms (R.V. righteousness [3]) before men, to be seen of them : otherwise, ye have no reward of your Father which is in heaven."

Finally, notwithstanding the great importance which Muhammed attaches to the duty of almsgiving, yet he does not forget to remind his followers that it is possible

[1] Cf. Christ's teaching in Luke 11, 41 : "But rather give alms of such things as ye have (τὰ ἐνόντα) ; and, behold, all things are clean unto you." Here Christ enjoins alms as the true means of purifying material objects for our use ; it is a counterpart to the ceremonial washings of the Pharisees. See Hastings "D. B." art. "Almsgiving."

[2] يُكَفِّرْ عَنْكُمْ مِنْ سَيِّآتِكُمْ. Cf. Sûras 5, 70 and 11, 116 : also Lane, Lex, under كَفَّرَ.

[3] See the commentaries on the passage. Although dikaiosunê is not used specifically for almsgiving in the Apocrypha nor in the Sept, yet the references to almsgiving and works of righteousness, such as we find in Tob. 2, 14, etc., show a strong association of ideas between them. Also we notice in the Qorân the contrast between "the believers who work righteousness" and "the unbelievers who give not alms."

to forfeit the promised reward through unworthy conduct. So we read in Sûra 2, 265 f. :—

> "Kind words and pardon are better than almsgiving followed by mischief. O ye believers, make not your alms of non-effect through reproaches and injury, like him who spendeth his substance to be seen of men, and believeth not in God and the last day. . . . No profit from their works shall they be able to gain; for God guideth not the unbelieving people."

Thus we find, on the one hand, that the prophet of Islâm, like the doctors of the Talmud, indisputably teaches the doctrine that almsgiving makes atonement for sin, a doctrine which is against the letter and the whole spirit of the New Testament. Still, one cannot be surprised at such a doctrine, since nothing is found in the Qorân corresponding to the N.T. teaching on the death of Christ as a sin-offering. On the other hand, Muhammed warns his followers against the thought that the fulfilment of this duty gives them a licence to live unworthy lives. Rather it is only when this virtue is accompanied by such others as adorn human life that the giver has his reward.[1]

[1] References to almsgiving will be found in the following sûras—2, 4, 9, 12, 13, 14, 16, 17, 19, 21, 22, 23, 24, 27, 30, 31, 32, 33, 34, 35, 36, 42, 57, 58, 69, 73, 74, 76, 98, 107.

E. LAWS CONCERNING MURDER AND THEFT

In this section we have the following matters to consider :—

1. *Intentional, or wilful murder.*
2. *Unintentional murder.*
3. *The* Lex Talionis, *or Retaliation.*
4. *Theft.*
5. *The slaying of female children.*

We shall first of all give a number of passages out of the Qorân, and then treat each matter in the above order.

Sûra 2, 173 ff. :—" O ye believers, retaliation for the slain is prescribed to you; the free for the free, the slave for the slave, the female for the female. But he to whom his brother shall make any remission, is to be dealt with equitably, and made to pay with liberality. This is an alleviation from your Lord, and a mercy; and he who transgresses after that shall suffer a grievous punishment. For you in retaliation is there life, O ye of understanding! it may be ye will fear."

Sûra 4, 94 f. :—" It is not for a believer to kill a believer save by mistake; and whosoever killeth a believer by mistake, shall be bound to free a believer from slavery; and the blood-money must be paid to his people, save what they shall remit as alms. But if the slain believer be of a hostile people, then let him set free a believing captive; and if he be of a people between whom and yourselves there is an alliance, then let the blood-money be paid to his family; and let him set free a slave who is a believer. And let him who hath not the means fast for two consecutive months. This is the penance from God. . . . But whoever shall kill a believer purposely, his reward is hell; for ever shall he abide therein; and God will be wrath with him, and curse him, and prepare for him a great torment."

Sûra 17, 35:—"And slay no one whom God hath forbidden you to slay, except for a just cause. And whosoever shall be slain wrongfully, we have given his next of kin power (to avenge him). But let him not go beyond bounds in putting to death; verily, he is ever helped." [1]

Sûra 22, 59:—"Whoever punishes with the like of what he has been injured with, and shall then be outraged again, God shall surely help him."

Sûra 42. In this sûra are given some of the characteristics of the true believers, where, among other things, they are said to be those—

v. 37:—"Who when an injury is done them, avenge themselves, yet let the recompense of evil be only a like evil. But he who forgiveth, and maketh peace, shall receive his reward from God. For He loveth not those who act unjustly. And whoso shall avenge himself after he hath been wronged, as to these, there is no way against them. Only shall there be a way open against those who unjustly wrong others, and act insolently on the earth in disregard of justice. These shall suffer a grievous punishment. And whoso beareth wrongs with patience, and forgiveth, verily, he doeth a work that is necessary."

The same subject is treated at the end of Sûra 16.

v. 127:—"If ye make reprisals, then make them to the same extent that ye were injured. But if ye can endure patiently, best will it surely be for the patiently enduring."

Words bearing further on retaliation are found in

Sûra 5, 49:—"And therein [2] have we enacted for them, Life for life, an eye for an eye, and nose for

[1] See Baidawi, *ad loc.*

[2] Ex. 21, 23 ff.

nose, and ear for ear, and tooth for tooth, and for wounds retaliation. But whoso remitteth it as alms, shall have therein the expiation of his sin." [1]

Finally, in the same Sûra (v. 42) we have the only reference that is made in the Qorân to theft :—

"The man thief and the woman thief, cut off the hands of both, as a punishment for their crime,—an example from God; for God is mighty and wise." [2]

It will be seen from the foregoing quotations that Muhammed lays great stress upon the duty of exercising moderation in the carrying out of the *lex talionis*; and this, apart from other evidence, shows to what extremes the fiery disposition of the Arabs carried them in the fulfilment of this duty. But this matter will be treated more fully further on. We will now consider each subject in the following order.

1. Intentional, or Wilful Murder

The punishment to be inflicted for this crime is death. The free shall die for the free, the slave for the slave, and a female for a female. These words, however, are not to be taken too strictly; for, according to the Sunna law, a man shall be put to death also for the murder of a woman. Also by the Hanafee law a man is liable to be so punished for the murder of another man's slave. But, on the other hand, a man who kills his own child or other descendant, or his own slave, or his son's slave, or a slave of whom he is part owner, is, according to

[1] فَهُوَ كَفَّارَةٌ لَهُ Lane (Lex) says, "The word denotes an act, or quality which has the effect of effacing a wrong action or sin or crime; that which covers or conceals sins or crimes; an expiation such as an almsgiving, and a fasting and the like." See also "KAT³," 601 f. and "Ges," (ed. 14) under כפר I.

[2] It is said that El-Walîd ben el-Mugira, a judge at Mecca, was the first to take cognizance of this law. See Wüstenfeld, "Genealogischen Tabellen," p. 461.

the Hanafee law, exempted from this punishment; and so also are his accomplices. Regard is also to be had to a difference in religion, so that a Muhammedan, though a slave, shall not be put to death for the murder of an unbeliever, though he be a freeman.

We also see that, in addition to suffering the penalty of death at the hands of his fellow-men, the slayer of a believer shall be made to suffer the most severe penalties in the next life. So we read:—

> "Whoever shall kill a believer purposely, his reward is hell; for ever shall he abide therein."

The verb employed here—خلد, means "to remain," "continue," "dwell long or endlessly in a place" (perennavit et sempiternus fuit—Freytag). It is, however, a doctrine of the Muhammedan religion that none who profess that faith shall remain in hell for ever; and so by some the term is taken to mean "a long duration of time." Others take the words in the sense of "He shall remain there for ever unless he repents."

It is further to be noticed that satisfaction for murder may be made through the payment of a certain sum of money to the family of the slain person.

However, the next of kin [1] may, if he will, refuse to accept a fine, and demand that the murderer be handed over into his hands. On the other hand, having once accepted a money payment, he is strictly forbidden to take any revenge on the murderer in future.

As we have seen, a peculiar characteristic of this law concerning wilful murder is, that it may be compounded for by a money payment. In the Old Testament legislation, on the other hand, there is nothing upon which greater stress is laid than the enactment that a murderer should be put to death. Again and again do we meet with the words, "the man-slayer shall surely be put to

[1] That is, the גֹּאֵל הַדָּם blood-avenger. See "Ges." (ed. 14), under גאל.

death." [1] No satisfaction was, on any account, to be taken for the life of a murderer. For this crime, which was looked upon as one of the most odious and abominable, there was to be no pardon, no pity :—

> "Thine eye shall not pity him, but thou shalt put away the innocent blood from Israel, that it may go well with thee." [2]

For the murderer the cities of refuge furnished no asylum; and he was dragged away even from the altar.[3]

Among the ancient Egyptians also wilful murder, even of a slave, was punishable with death; and the witness thereof who did not try to prevent the crime was similarly punished.[4]

In the Roman laws we find nine crimes enumerated as being considered worthy of death as punishment, one of which is the wilful murder of a citizen, for which, says Gibbon,[5] the common feelings of mankind demand the blood of the murderer.

On the other hand, in the Homeric world the case is exactly the same as what we find in the Qorân. The life of a man-slayer was forfeited to the kinsman of the slain, who might, however, accept a fine (ποινή) as satisfaction; and we read, also, of men guilty of manslaughter or wilful murder going into exile.[6]

We have seen that the prophet, in formulating his enactments, had regard to the different classes of society.[7] And this distinction is one that is generally recognized, as, for example, in the Old Testament, where we read, Ex. 21, 20 :—

[1] Cf. Num., chap. 35.
[2] Deut. 19, 13.
[3] Ex. 21, 14; 1 Kings 2, 28 ff.
[4] Bettany, "The World's Religions," p. 480.
[5] Gibbon, "Roman Empire," vol. 3, p. 241.
[6] See Jebb's "Homer," p. 54. Also cf. the Hebrew law, according to which the slayer was obliged to remain in the city of refuge until the death of the high priest (*i.e.*, the unintentional slayer only).
[7] Cf. Sûra 2, 173.

> "If a man smite his servant, or his maid, with a rod, and he die under his hand; he shall surely be punished."

That is, "Vengeance shall surely be taken."[1] But it is not explained of what this vengeance was to consist. The Jewish commentators maintain that he was to suffer death by the sword. In that case, however, we would expect the usual expression מוֹת יוּמַת. Probably it was left to the authorities to determine the mode of punishment according to the circumstances.

And the same distinction is found also in Hammurabi, cf. § 116 :—

> "If the distress has died in the house of his distrainer, of blows or of want, the owner of the distress shall put his merchant to account; and if he be the son of a freeman (that has died), his son one shall kill; if the slave of a freeman, he shall pay one-third of a mina of silver, and he shall lose all that he gave, whatever it be."[2]

2. Unintentional Murder, or Manslaughter

In this case several distinctions are made, as :—

(*a*) Where a believing Moslim slay another believer, who is of his own people. The penalty in this case is the freeing of a believer from captivity, and the payment of a certain sum to the family of the slain person.

(*b*) Where a believer slays another believer, but where the people of the slayer and the slain are at enmity with each other. Here the penalty is the freeing of a believer from captivity. But no fine is to be imposed in addition as in the former case. The reason for this is, that the tribe to which the slain person belongs are unbelievers.

(*c*) Where the slain person belongs to a people that are in confederacy with the Moslims. The penalty in this

[1] נָקֹם יִנָּקֵם.

[2] The same distinction will be seen also in §§ 218 f., 230 f., 251 f., etc.

case is the same as in the first, namely, the freeing of a believer from captivity, and a money payment. In those cases where the slayer has not the means to pay the required sum, he is commanded to fast for two consecutive months.

As regards the amount of the above fine, which is the price of blood, according to the Sunna law it is a hundred camels, or a thousand deenars (about £500) from him who possesses gold, or twelve thousand dirhems (about £300) from him who possesses silver. This is the fine for the killing of a free man. For a woman it is half this sum, and for a slave it is his or her value; but that must fall short of the price of blood for the free.[1]

In cases of manslaughter the law of the Qorân provides nothing corresponding to what we find in the Mosaic Code, namely, the cities of refuge. As we have seen, unintentional murder is to be expiated for with a fine and the freeing of a captive Moslim. It is noteworthy, however, that in many cases where the Muhammedan laws differ from those of the Old Testament, they agree substantially with those of Hammurabi. We have here another instance of this. In Hammurabi, § 206 ff., we read :—

> "If a man has struck a man in a quarrel, and has caused him a wound, that man shall swear, 'I did not strike him with knowledge' (or intentionally), and shall pay the doctor. If he die of his blows, he shall swear, and if he be of gentle birth he shall pay half a mina of silver, etc."

In some cases, however, the Hammurabi law of manslaughter is very severe, especially where death has been caused through neglect (cf. § 229 ff.).

3. *Lex Talionis*, or Retaliation

As we have seen from our quotations, Muhammed allows retaliation to his followers. And it is necessary

[1] See Lane, "Modern Egyptians," p. 119.

that something further should be said upon this matter.

Reference has already been made to the cities of refuge among the Israelites. The establishment of these cities presupposed the custom and right of revenge. The custom itself goes back to the earliest times. It prevailed, not only among the Israelites and the Arabs, but also among most, if not all, of the other nations of antiquity.[1] Revenge of blood prevailed almost everywhere, so long as there was no national life generated, or it was still in the first stages of its development. Consequently the expiation of any personal violation of justice was left to private revenge, and more especially to family zeal. The warrant for this may be said to be the principle of retribution, the jus talionis, which lay at the foundation of the divine order of the world.

The practice of blood revenge was carried on among the Arabs in all its fierceness. With them the idea of kinship in blood to the god of their tribe was a predominant factor, which made the blood of a kinsman holy and inviolable, and sanctioned the extremes of blood revenge. Consequently this blood revenge was with them a religious duty. The shedding of blood, whether intentional or not, whether in peace or war, was a crime to be avenged. This duty was incumbent upon the next of kin, the go'el. But in the fulfilment of his duty he was not left alone; the whole clan would take his part. This again would be followed by the clan of the murderer taking his part, and this would lead to an incessant war between the two clans, that of the slayer and that of the slain; and every murder committed during this feud would supply a cause for new revenge.

As we have already remarked, murder, like other crimes, may be compounded for by a money payment, or rather, the handing over of so many camels. This is brought about through an agreement between the slayer

[1] See art. "Goel" in Hastings "D.B.," where also at the end a valuable list of books on the subject will be found.

and the family of the slain, or between the two clans concerned. When this agreement has been made, the cause of the feud is naturally removed. But even when compensation has been made, animosity frequently continues between the two parties for a long time. It is not likely that among a people of the temper of the Arabs feelings roused by what they regard as the greatest of crimes would be soon calmed, even though compensation has been made.

Our quotations from the Qorân show, further, that retaliation is allowed also by the prophet for wounds. It is "life for life, eye for an eye, nose for a nose, ear for an ear, tooth for a tooth, and for wounds retaliation."

If it be urged that Muhammed could not have abolished the custom of revenge in the case of murder, still he could certainly have insisted upon the entire abolition of it in the case of minor crimes. It is not to his credit that he has given his sanction to such a cruel custom as had already been abolished by the Christian dispensation.

It may be asked, did Muhammed intend that this expression, "life for life, eye for an eye," etc., should be taken literally. Sale [1] maintains that these words, both in the Qorân and in the Old Testament, are not to be so understood. He says, "The expression 'eye for eye, and tooth for tooth' being only a proverbial manner of speaking, the sense whereof amounts to this, that every one shall be punished by the judges according to the heinousness of the fact." Sale says further, "The talio, likewise established among the old Romans by the laws of the twelve tables, was not to be inflicted, unless the delinquent could not agree with the person injured." [2]

But there seems to be no reason for taking the expression, either in the Qorân or in the Old Testament, other

[1] Prel. Discourse, Sect. 6, and note.

[2] Gibbon says: "They approve the inhuman and unequal principle of retaliation; and the forfeit of an eye for an eye, a tooth for a tooth, a limb for a limb is rigorously exacted, unless the offender can redeem his pardon by a fine of three hundred pounds of copper." "Roman Empire," vol. 3, p. 241.

than in its strict literal sense as teaching perfect retaliation. For example, in Ex. 21, after referring to those cases where a money payment may be made, the author proceeds (v. 23) :—

> " But if any mischief follow, then thou shalt give life for life, eye for eye, tooth for tooth, hand for hand, foot for foot, burning for burning, wound for wound, stripe for stripe." [1]

Although, however, Muhammed himself says nothing as to a money payment in the case of wounds, this is allowed by the Muhammedan jurists, the amount being as follows :—

For a member of the body that is single, such as a nose, the whole price of blood, as in the case of murder.

For a member of which there are two, and not more, such as a hand, half the price of blood.

For a member of which there are ten, *i.e.*, a finger or a toe, a tenth of the price of blood.

When a man maims or wounds a woman, the fine is half of that for the same injury to a man.

When a free man wounds a slave, the fine varies according to the value of the slave.

When a man is deprived of any of his five senses, or is dangerously wounded, or is grievously disfigured for life, the fine is the whole price of blood.

Thus we see that by the Muhammedan law all these different crimes, namely, wilful murder, manslaughter (unintentional), and personal injury may, without exception, be met by a fine. In this respect this law is certainly unique; at any rate, we know of no other legal code, either ancient or modern, where this manner of satisfying justice is made possible to such an extent. In the case of murder, both premeditated and unpremeditated,

[1] Of course, it does not follow that the Jews did insist upon this full retaliation, at least, in later times. In the Mishna we read : " If a man has blinded another, or cut off his hand, or broken his foot, one must regard the injured person as though he were a slave sold in the market, and put a price upon him, and reckon how much he was worth before the injury, and how much now."

this is allowed by Muhammed himself in the Qorân; and, as we have seen, by the Moslim doctors it is extended to the cases of personal injury.

Further, we notice that Muhammed also, quite in agreement with the great stress which he lays on almsgiving, favours the remitting as alms the penalty enacted by him for injury. He says (Sûra 5, 49):—

> "Wounds should be punished by retaliation; but whoso remits it (as alms), it is an expiation for him."

In fixing the amount of the fine, regard must be taken of the status, not only of the victim (that is, whether he be a freeman or a slave), but also of that of the offender (whether he be a rich man or a poor man). This, however, is a distinction observed by other legislators, and is one that would naturally be expected.[1]

Although we believe that the prophet could have done much more than he did in order to abolish the cruel custom of retaliation, still when we remember to what extremes the Arabs went in the fulfilment of this duty, it must be confessed that Muhammed took a step in the right direction. His attempt, as far as it goes, was praiseworthy. But the evil here, as in most of his other enactments, is that what he has commanded is to hold good for all times.

I shall bring this subject to a close with a saying of Abu Hanifat, which expresses his wish that the desire for revenge on the part of the Arabs should be curbed. "It is related of the Imâm Abu Hanifat that he was asked concerning a man who struck a man with a stone, and killed him, whether retaliation was necessary, and he answered, no, not even if he had struck him with Abu Qubais."[2]

[1] In the Mosaic code the *lex talionis* applied only to the free Israelite. In the case of slaves, if the master struck out an eye and destroyed it, *i.e.*, blinded him with the blow, or struck out a tooth, he was to let him go free, as a compensation for the loss of the member. See Ex. 21, 26 f.

[2] The name of a mountain near Mecca. From Košut, "Fünf Streitfragen der Basrenser und Kûfenser," p. 72.

4. Theft

Rightly or wrongly, the Arabs have long been regarded as a people unequalled in the practice of stealing. Writer after writer relates how the genial Arab relieves the unfortunate traveller of what he has, and repeats the grounds upon which the sons of the desert seek to justify this general failing:—

"Robbery and murder were their ordinary occupations, for an Arab looked on work or agriculture as beneath his dignity, and thought that he had a prescriptive right to the property of those who condescended to such mean offices." [1]

Although we may regard this description of the Arabs as somewhat exaggerated, still it seems strange that the matter of theft, which is so fully treated by other legislators, should receive such scant notice by Muhammed.

As we have already seen, theft is only *once* referred to in the Qorân, and that in a very few words:—

> "The man thief and the woman thief, cut off the hands of both, as a punishment for their crime;—an example from God, for God is mighty and wise."

It will be well for us, however, to refer to some of the enactments of the Muhammedan lawyers, who treat the subject with the fulness it demands.

The law enacts that, for a first offence, the right hand shall be cut off; for a second, the left foot; and should the man steal a third time, he shall undergo a long term of imprisonment, that is, until he shall reform. Some maintain that for a third offence the culprit's left hand should be cut off, and for a fourth offence, his right foot. The school of Abu Hanifat, however, is not of this opinion, since Ali, the prophet's son-in-law, had said that he would be ashamed before God that a man could not after wards take anything, because he had no hands, nor could he go about, because he had no feet.

[1] E. H. Palmer, "The Qur'ân," Intro., p. x.

The hand of the thief is to be cut off at the wrist. But this shall not take place if the other hand has already been cut off, or is useless; or if the thumb or two fingers of the other hand has been cut off, or again the right hand is crippled. It is also enacted that this mutilation shall not take place during great heat or cold.

Before any of these punishments can be inflicted the following proofs are required:—

(*a*) That two male witnesses give their testimony against the accused, or that he himself confesses his guilt. It is open to the accused to withdraw his confession, and to flee from punishment is regarded as a retraction. The judge must be satisfied as to what has been stolen, where and when the theft took place, the value of the thing or things stolen, and to whom it or they belonged. It is necessary to inquire into these questions also even when a confession has been made, with the exception of that of time, since the prescription comes not into account when the thief himself confesses.

(*b*) That the value of the goods stolen be not less than a quarter of a deenár.

(*c*) A thief's hand shall not be cut off for the theft of what cannot be guarded, or is not worth guarding, being found in the land in great quantity, such as dry wood, hay, grass, reeds, game, fish, lime, etc.; also such articles of food as are quickly perishable, as milk, meat, fresh fruit, etc. Further, a man may not be punished for stealing from his wife, or the wife from her husband, even if the husband has his goods under special care. Neither is a slave to be punished who steals from his master, or his master's wife; nor the guest who steals from his host, or he who steals from the house of a near relative, even if the thing stolen should belong to another. On the other hand, should a thief bring disgrace or harm upon his relatives through entering the house of another, his hand is to be cut off.

(*d*) Finally, the thief's hand shall not be cut off if the thing stolen hath no commercial value, even though it be otherwise regarded as of great worth. Of such may be regarded intoxicating spirits, provided no harm shall follow to a Muhammedan. So also is the theft of playthings (*i.e.*, cards, etc.), and crosses, even if made from gold, as well as copies of the Qorân, and the children of free people, who are recognized as such, because they are not regarded as property. But the theft of a slave is punishable.

Many other cases are treated by the Muhammedan doctors which we must pass over.

As we have seen, the usual punishment for theft, both according to the Qorân and the Muhammedan jurists is mutilation.[1] This is not only a cruel punishment, but is also in the highest degree unreasonable. For, while many acts of theft may be attributed to want, a man's chances of earning an honest living are naturally lessened when he is deprived of one or more of his members. Further, although this barbarous mode of punishment is not confined to Muhammedan countries,[2] still it stands in contrast with what may be regarded as the usual mode of punishment for this crime among the ancients, which was either restitution or death.

Among the Hebrews, except in certain cases, the thief was compelled to make restitution. This varied in amount, rising as the means of detection became more difficult.[3] Thus, if a stolen animal were found alive in a man's possession, he was to restore two-fold; but if it had been already slain or sold, he was to pay five oxen for an ox, and four sheep for a sheep. If the thief did

[1] Lane (" Modern Egyptians," chap. 3) says: " In Egypt, of late years, these punishments have not been inflicted. Beating and hard labour have been substituted for the first, second, or third offence, and frequently death for the fourth. Most petty offences are usually punished by beating with the " kurbág " (a thong or whip of hippopotamus's hide, hammered into a round form), or with a stick, generally on the soles of the feet."

[2] Cf. Hammurabi, § 253: " If a man has hired a man to reside in his field, and has furnished him seed, has entrusted him the oxen and harnessed them for cultivating the field—if that man has stolen the corn or plants, and they have been seized in his hands, one shall cut off his hands."

[3] Ex., chap. 22.

not make restitution, they seized what was in his house, put it up for sale, and even sold the man himself, if he had not wherewith to make satisfaction.

As we have already seen, a thief's hand shall not be cut off if he steal such stuffs as are quickly perishable, since it is possible that he took them owing to hunger. With this we may compare Prov. 6, 30 f.:—

> "Men do not despise a thief if he steal to satisfy his soul when he is hungry. (31) But if he be found, he shall restore sevenfold; he shall give all the substance of his house." [1]

Also by the Roman law a man pursued and recovered his stolen goods by a civil action of theft; they were restored by the sentence of the praetor, and the injury was compensated for by double, or threefold, or even fourfold damages, according as the deed had been perpetrated by secret fraud or open rapine, or as the robber had been surprised in the act, or detected by a subsequent research.[2]

On the other hand, in certain cases, a thief was punished with death, as, for instance, in the case of a nocturnal thief. In this the Hebrew, Athenian, and Roman laws agree, as does also that of Hammurabi, as we read in § 21:—

> "If a man has broken into a house, one shall kill him before the breach, and bury him in it." [3]

Another crime punishable with death by both the Hammurabi (§ 14 ff.) and the Hebrew codes is man-stealing. I shall give only the following passages:—

> Ex. 21, 16. "He that stealeth a man, and selleth him, or if he be found in his hand, he shall surely be put to death."

[1] Rather, "he may restore . . . he may give all," etc. The law only knows of a twofold, fourfold, fivefold restoration (cf. Ex., chap. 22); but a man may give more. See "Del. Comm.," *ad loc.*

[2] See Gibbon, "Roman Empire," vol. 3, 240.

[3] In general, the Hammurabi laws against theft are very severe, death being the penalty in most cases. Cf. § 6 ff., § 22, § 25.

Deut. 24, 7. "If a man be found stealing any of his brethren of the children of Israel, and he deal with him as a slave, or sell him; then that thief shall die."

It will be seen that the reference here is to the theft of a free Israelite. The Hebrews did not believe that the theft of a foreigner deserved death, but only the theft of one of the children of Israel. If it were a stranger that was stolen, the punishment was restitution.

Finally, we notice that men-stealers are placed by St. Paul (1 Tim. 1, 10) also among the greatest miscreants.

To sum up, the Muhammedan law of theft is by no means such as to command our praise; on the contrary, it is, as already said, a cruel and unreasonable enactment. And the same must be said of the laws enacted by the Muhammedan doctors, in whose works we also find much of what can only be described as absurd.[1]

It will be seen that I have referred to the subject of theft, as it is dealt with in different codes, rather fully. This was from a desire to show, on the one hand, how insufficiently the matter is treated by Muhammed himself in the Qorân, and, on the other hand, the peculiar character of the punishments enacted by the Muhammedan doctors as compared with those we generally find in other ancient codes.

5. Slaying of Female Children

Before I bring this section to a close, I shall refer briefly to a cruel custom which obtained among some of the Arab tribes in pre-Islamic times, and to which Muhammed refers several times in the Qorân, namely, the slaying of female children. This inhuman practice is strongly condemned by the prophet, as the following quotations show:—

Sûra 6, 138:—"Thus too have their associates made seemly to many of the idolators the killing of their

[1] Such as, for instance, their definition of a "proper place," for different things, from which to steal them is punishable. See Krcsmárik in "Z.D.M.G." (1904), p. 326 f.

children, that they might destroy them, and make obscure for them their religion." [1]

Sûra 16, 60 f. :—" When any one of them has tidings of a female child, his face is overclouded and black, and he has to keep back his wrath. He skulks away from the people, for the evil tidings he has heard;—Is he to keep it with its disgrace, or to bury it in the dust? "

Sûra 17, 33 :—" Slay not your children for fear of poverty; we will provide for them. Verily to slay them is a great sin."

Sûra 81, 9 :—" And when the child who was buried alive shall be asked for what sin she was slain."

It will be seen from the foregoing quotations that two reasons were assigned for this custom, namely :—

(*a*) The fear of being reduced to poverty through having to provide for such children.

(*b*) To avoid the disgrace which would follow, if they should happen to be taken captive, or to become scandalous through their loose behaviour. Consequently, the birth of a daughter was regarded as a great misfortune, and the death of one as an unmixed blessing. Probably, however, the second reason given was a mere pretence, and the real reason for the existence of the custom was poverty. It is well known that the nomadic Arabs suffered much from want during a great part of the year. The rich alone had sufficient to eat, and these gave the protection of their honour as the reason for the slaying of their daughters. But to the poor a daughter was naturally a burden, and so, in their battle for existence, this custom did not appear to them to be improper, as was the case with other uneducated peoples. Further, we find that this burying alive of female children was not the only device of the ancient Arabs in order to check the growth of the population among them.[2]

[1] Some think that this passage refers to the practice of sacrificing children to idols (Baidawi, *ad loc*).

[2] See " Kinship and Marriage," p. 153 ff., and add. note c: also Lane (Lex.) under عزل, and Al-Harîrî, " Durrat-al-Gawwas," p. 6 f.

It must be remembered, however, that this cruel custom prevailed among only a few of the Arabic tribes; it was by no means a general thing with them. Consequently we have here something against which the prophet could speak out boldly, without fear of much opposition.

As we have seen, this practice was by no means confined to the Arabs. On the contrary, it was a very general custom among the ancients. Indeed it is noticed as a very remarkable thing among the Egyptians that they brought up *all* their children. While, on the other hand, in the "Book of Actions and Retributions" of the Taoists we find the enactment, "Do not kill your children, either before or after birth." [1] And it is well known that even at the present day, this custom is practised among the Chinese with impunity.

Nor must it be thought that this custom was confined to the Orient. In early Greece, by the law of Lycurgus, no child was to be brought up without the approbation of public officers. "The moment a Spartan was born, the state began to take cognizance of him. The infant was carried before the elders, who decided on his fate; if healthy, he was taken back to his parents, to be reared; if weakly, he was taken away and cast out on Taÿgetus, to perish by exposure." [2] Here, however, it will be seen that the reason for this procedure was totally different from those referred to above, the laws being framed with the sole view to the building up of a strong military state.

The same custom prevailed also among the Romans. Gibbon [3] says:—

> "The same protection was due to every period of existence; and reason must applaud the humanity of Paulus for imputing the crime of murder to

[1] Bettany, "The World's Religions," p. 156.
[2] C. W. C. Oman, "History of Greece," p. 69. (Longmans, Green and Co., London, 1898.)
[3] "Roman Empire," Vol. 3, p. 225 f.

the father who strangles or starves or abandons his new-born infant, or exposes him in a public place, to find the mercy which he himself had denied. But the exposition of children was the prevailing and stubborn vice of antiquity; it was sometimes prescribed, often permitted, almost always practised with impunity, by the nations who never entertained the Roman ideas of paternal powers; and the dramatic poets, who appeal to the human hearts, represent with indifference a popular custom which was palliated by the motives of economy and compassion. If the father could subdue his own feelings, he might escape, though not the censure, at least the chastisement of the laws; and the Roman Empire was stained with the blood of infants, till such murders were included by Valentinian and his colleagues in the letter and spirit of the Cornelian law. The lessons of jurisprudence and Christianity had been insufficient to eradicate this inhuman practice, till their gentle influence was fortified by the terrors of capital punishment."

This custom, then, which, as we have seen, was practised among many nations both in the East and West, was strongly denounced by Muhammed, and so in Arabia came to an end. Customs that are old, and very generally practised among a people, die hard. But in this case, however old the practice might have been with the Arabs, it was by no means general, and hence its abolition was not so difficult as it otherwise would have been. None the less does Muhammed deserve our praise for what he did.

F. LAWS RELATING TO COMMERCIAL MATTERS

While some of the Arabs led a nomadic life, obtaining their living from the rearing of camels, horses, cattle, and sheep, others were engaged in commerce;[1] and their caravans set out at regular intervals to the East and West. In Sûra 106 we read :—

> " For the uniting of the Qoraish; uniting them for the caravan of winter and summer;[2] let them serve the Lord of this house, who feeds them against hunger, and makes them safe against fear."

The Western caravan route was in use in the prophet's time; and Hashim, his great-grandfather, died at Gaza when on a mercantile expedition to Syria. And, as is well known, Muhammed himself was also engaged for some years in commerce.

References to this subject are found scattered throughout the Qorân, from which we learn that the legitimacy of commerce is fully recognized by the prophet, provided it be carried on in an honest and straightforward manner. We shall first of all give a few passages in which the matter is dealt with in a general way, and then proceed to discuss the various points separately.

In Sûra 2, Muhammed speaks concerning the pilgrimage to Mecca, and gives several directions in connection therewith, one of which reads :—

> " It is no crime to you that ye seek good from your Lord; but when ye pour forth from 'Arafat, remember God by the sacred beacon."

[1] Cf. Ezek. 27, 21. Also art. " Arabia " in Hastings, " D.B."
[2] In winter to Yemen and in summer to Syria (Baidawi).

Thus permission is given to the Muhammedans to engage in commerce even during the pilgrimage, a permission which we have no doubt they took full advantage of. Again in Sûra 4, 33 :—

> " O believers, consume not each others' wealth in mutual frivolities, unless there be trafficking among you by your own consent."
>
> Sûra 30, 45 :—" And one of his signs is, that He sendeth the winds with glad tidings, that he may cause you to taste his mercy, and that ships may sail at his command, that out of his bounties ye may seek wealth." [1]

While, however, full permission is thus given to trade, even when on pilgrimage; yet, as we learn from another Sûra, the zeal with which the Arabs of the prophet's time gave themselves up to this was not altogether pleasing to him. He was much grieved to find them, on the approach of a caravan, withdrawing en masse, leaving him to preach to empty seats. So we read in Sûra 62, 9 ff. :—

> " O believers, when the call to prayer is made, upon the day of the assembly,[2] then hasten to the remembrance of God, and leave off traffic; that is better for you, if ye did but know. And when prayer is performed, then disperse abroad in the land, and seek of the bounties of God; and remember God much; haply ye may prosper. But when they see merchandise or sport, they flock to it, and leave thee standing. Say, ' What is with God is better than sport and than merchandise, for God is the best of providers."

[1] الرزق بالتجارة في البحر - من فضله " Sustenance through trade on the sea." Galalaiṇ.

[2] That is, Friday, called يوم الجمعة the day of the assembly. It was formerly called يوم العروبة (see Lane, Lex). It was the day on which Muhammed entered Medina for the first time.

We will now notice the several matters in the following order, (*a*) Contracts, (*b*) Debts, (*c*) Usury, (*d*) Weights and Measures, (*e*) Bribery.

(*a*) *Contracts.* Sûra 5 opens with the words:—

"O believers, perform your contracts."

Also in Sûra 23, 8, we are told that the true believers are those "who tend well their trusts and covenants." In Sûra 2 the matter is treated more fully; v. 283 f. reads:—

> "If it be a present bargain which ye transact between yourselves, it shall be no crime in you if ye write it not down. And take witnesses when ye sell one to the other, and let no harm be done to the writer nor to the witnesses, which if ye do, will be injustice in you. . . . And if ye be on a journey, and cannot find a writer, then let a pledge be taken. But if one of you trust another, then let him who is trusted return what he is trusted with, and let him fear God his Lord. And conceal not the testimony, for he who conceals it hath surely a wicked heart."

Here Muhammed impresses upon his followers the duty of strictly fulfilling their contracts, and gives directions as to the mode of procedure under different circumstances.

(i) When a contract or bargain is made, the parties concerned may or may not commit the same to writing. All such transactions are to take place in the presence of witnesses. Although the prophet does not say so, we may take it that two witnesses at least are necessary, as in the case of debts, etc. Further, Muhammed speaks against the molesting of such persons as write down the contracts, or are witnesses thereto, a thing which such persons are always open to.

(ii) If the parties concerned be on a journey, and no writer available, the one may give to the other a pledge. But in cases where the parties are well known to each other, and have implicit faith in each other's honesty, no such pledge is necessary.

(*b*) *Debts.* In Sûra 2 is treated also the question of debts. Muhammed urges his followers to deal leniently with those who are in financial difficulties. "If," says Bosworth Smith,[1] "the two social touchstones of a religion are the way in which, relatively to the time, it deals with the weaker sex, and the way in which it regards the poor and the oppressed, Mohammed's religion can stand the test." That the prophet did much to put down injustice and oppression, no one can deny; and in his enactments concerning the treatment of debtors we have another proof of this. I give the following quotations:—

Sûra 2, 280:—"If anyone be in difficulties (regarding a debt), then wait for easy circumstances: but that ye remit it as alms is better for you, if ye did but know."

Id. v. 282:—"O ye believers, if ye engage to one another in a debt for a stated time, then write it down; and let a scribe write it down between you faithfully; nor let a scribe refuse to write as God taught him, but let him write, and let him who owes dictate. But let him fear God his Lord, and not diminish therefrom aught. But if he who owes be foolish, or weak, or cannot dictate himself, then let his agent dictate faithfully; and let them call two witnesses out from amongst their men; or if there be not two men, then a man and two women, from those whom he chooses for witnesses, so that if one of the two should err, the second of the two may remind the other. And let not the witnesses refuse when they are summoned; and let them not distain to write it, be it large or small, with its time of payment. This will be more just for you in the sight of God, better suited for testimony, and the best for avoiding doubt."

It will thus be seen that Muhammed is very lenient towards debtors. Nothing is said in the Qorân itself regarding the punishment of debtors. The "law," however, ordains that a debtor shall be imprisoned for

[1] "Mohammed and Mohammedanism," p. 175.

the non-payment of his debt. But if he can establish his insolvency he is to be liberated. Further, if in good health, he may be compelled to work for the discharge of his debt. But it must be remembered that no Muhammedan can be reduced to the position of a slave. That is strictly forbidden.

When we turn to the Old Testament enactments concerning debtors, we find that the position of an Israelite was by no means light. A debtor could be reduced to slavery; he was not, however, to be treated as an ordinary slave, but rather as an hired servant, and was to be released in the year of jubilee.[1] In later times we find an endeavour made to better the position of a debtor. He was to work for a certain time in order to wipe out his debt.[2]

With the above we compare Hammurabi, § 117 :—

> " If a man a debt has seized him, and he has given his wife, his son, his daughter, for the money, or has handed over to work off the debt, for three years they shall work in the house of their buyer or exploiter, in the fourth year he shall fix their liberty." [3]

We thus see that in this matter the Muhammedan teachers agree with both the Hebrew and Hammurabi codes. According to all of them a man was authorized to compel a debtor to work in order to wipe off his debt. Further, as we have seen, a Muhammedan debtor can be imprisoned. And from some passages in the New Testament we learn that imprisonment was the penalty in the time of Christ. Matt. 5, 25 f. reads :—

> " Agree with thine adversary quickly, whilst thou art with him in the way; lest haply the adversary deliver thee to the judge, and the judge deliver thee to the officer, and thou be cast into prison. Verily I say unto thee, Thou shalt by no means

[1] See Lev. 25, 39 ff., etc.
[2] See Ex. 21, 2; Deut. 15, 12; 2 Kings 4, 1.
[3] See also § 48, § 115 f., § 118 f.

come out thence, till thou have paid the last farthing." [1, 2]

In conclusion, we may say that the law of the Qorân as well as the enactments of the Muhammedan doctors, when compared with those of the Old Testament and of Hammurabi are lenient and just. And especially so when we further compare them with the Roman law of debt, according to which a debtor might even be put to death, and where the cruel exactions of creditors several times led to serious disturbances.[3]

(*c*) *Usury*. The question of usury naturally goes with that of debts and debtors. Usurers form one of the most despicable classes of men. Ben Jonson speaks of "usurious cannibals"; and Bishop Hall says: "See if there be any such tiger or wolf, as an enemy, as an usuring oppressor." And the practices of usurers are by Muhammed, as by other legislators, condemned in the severest terms. The matter is referred to several times in the Qorân. Sûra 2, 276 f., reads:—

"Those who devour usury [4] shall not rise again, save as he riseth whom Satan hath paralysed with a touch; [5] and that is because they say, 'Selling is only like usury'; but God hath made selling

[1] Cf. Matt. 18, 30.

[2] With the ancient Egyptians only goods could be seized for debt, the person being the property of the king or of the State. At an early period people were required to give in pledge for borrowed money the mummy of a father or some near relative, a deposit certain to be redeemed if at all possible; for if it were not redeemed the debtor could not be buried with the usual ceremonies, or in any honourable place.—Bettany, "The World's Religions," p. 480.

[3] See H. G. Liddell, "History of Rome" (John Murray, London, 1861), p. 73.

[4] The Hebrew word for usury is very characteristic, namely, נֶשֶׁךְ, a bite, sting, vb. נָשַׁךְ, Ass. mashâku, to bite. In Welsh the usual trans. is ocraeth (cf. Lev. 25, 36, etc.), which Prof. Sir J. Morris Jones, M.A., assures me is not a Welsh word. Possibly it is from some French form of lucre, where the l is mistaken for the art. Very significant also is the Greek word *τόκος*, lit. a bringing forth, birth. And so Shakespeare can speak of usurers as those who

"take a *breed* of barren metal."

[5] That is, in a convulsive agitation of body, which the Orientals attribute to the working of Satan.

lawful and usury unlawful; and he to whom the admonition from his Lord has come, if he desists, what has gone before is his; his matter is in God's hands. But whosoever returns (to usury), these are the fellows of the fire, and they shall dwell therein for ever. God shall blot out usury, but shall make almsgiving profitable; for God loves not any sinful unbeliever."

Id. v. 278 :—" O ye believers, fear God, and remit the balance of usury, if ye be believers. And if ye will not do it, then hearken to the proclamation of war from God and His apostle. But if ye repent, your capital is yours. Ye shall not wrong, nor shall ye be wronged."

Sûra 30, 38 :—" Whatever ye put out at usury to increase it with the substance of others, shall have no increase from God."

On the word رِبًا, or رِبوٌ, Lane (Lex) remarks as follows :

" An excess, and an addition; an addition over and above the principal sum (that is lent or expended); but in the law it signifies an addition obtained in a particular manner (*i. e.* usury and the like, meaning both unlawful and lawful, interest or profit, and the practice of taking such interest or profit); it is in lending, or in buying and selling, and in giving; and is of two kinds; unlawful and lawful; the unlawful is any loan for which one receives more than the loan, or by means of which one draws a profit; [and the gain made by such means]; and the lawful is a gift by which a man invites more than it to be given to him, or a gift that he gives in order that more than it may be given to him; [and the addition that he so obtains]. (It generally means) an addition that is obtained by selling food, etc., for food, etc., or ready money for ready money, to be paid at an appointed period; or by exchanging either of such things for more of the same kind." [1]

[1] Other words of a similar meaning are عَيْن, عِينَة, سَلَف. See also Ges.[14] under מַרְבִּית and for difference between נֶשֶׁךְ and מרבית see Del. on Prov. 28, 8.

Also in the Talmud (Baba "Mezi'â." chap. 5) usury is explained as follows: "What does usury mean? When anyone lends one sela (which is worth four dénars) for five dénars, or two seah of wheat for three seah; that is forbidden, because he bites; prop. the money or other lent goods which he takes through the paying back of a part of the debtor's property."

According to the passages quoted from the Qorân we learn that there shall be a double punishment for the practice of usury, namely, the loss of God's blessing in this world, and the torture of hell in the next. On the other hand, it will be seen that Muhammed leaves entirely open the question whether his followers may or may not practise usury with people of another religion. This is allowed by the Hebrew code,[1] and, as is well known, is taken advantage of to the full. But the practice of usury between the Israelites themselves is severely denounced in several passages of the Old Testament.[2] And not only do both the Hebrew and the Muhammedan legislators join in condemning usury, but also in connecting the giving or the withholding of God's blessing with the same.[3] It is more than probable, therefore, that Muhammed was conversant with the Old Testament teaching as regards usury.

(*d*) *Weights and Measures.* The use of unjust weights and measures is another matter which comes in for the prophet's condemnation, which shows that the Arabs no less than the Jews were guilty of fraudulent dealing. The following passages on the subject are found in the Qorân :—

Sûra 6, 153 :—" Use a full measure, and a just balance."

Sûra 7, 83 :—" Give good weight and measure, and be not niggardly of your gifts to men, and do not evil in the earth after it has been righted."

[1] Cf. Deut. 23, 20. "Unto a foreigner thou mayest lend upon usury."

[2] See Ex. 22, 25; Neh. 5, 7; Ps. 15, 5; Prov. 28, 8.

[3] Deut. 23, 20. See also Driver's "Deuteronomy," p. 265 ff.

Sûra 55, 6 ff. :—" He (God) hath appointed the balance, that in the balance ye should not transgress. Weigh, therefore, with fairness, and stint not the balance."

In Sûra 83, entitled " Those who give short weight," Muhammed uses strong words against such offenders:—

V. 1 ff. :—" Woe to those who give short weight! who when they measure against others take full measure; but when they measure to them or weigh to them, diminish. Do not these think that they shall be raised again at the great day, the day when men shall stand before the Lord of the worlds? By no means."

It will be seen that the words used by Islâm's legislator greatly resemble those found in the Old Testament, a fact which suggests an acquaintance with the latter on Muhammed's part. This unjust practice is forbidden in several places in the Pentateuch, and strongly condemned by the prophets in all periods of the nation's history.[1] Further, it would appear that the form which this frauding took was similar among the Jews and the Arabs. Thus in Deut. 25, 13 f., we read :—

" Thou shalt not have in thy bag divers weights,[2] a great and a small. Thou shalt not have in thine house divers measures, a great and a small."

The author means two kinds of stones, a large and a small, for weights, and two kinds of measures, a large and a small, that is, the large for buying, and the small for selling. And probably this is the meaning of the words in the Qorân (Sûra 83, 1 ff.) quoted above:

" . . . when they measure against others take full measure; but when they measure to them or weigh to them, diminish."

[1] Cf. Lev. 19, 36; Deut. 25, 13; Mic. 6, 11; Prov. 11, 1; 16, 11; 20, 10, 23; Am. 8, 5.

[2] Lit. אֶבֶן וָאֶבֶן—איפה וְאיפה. So also in Prov. 20, 10; cf. also Ps. 12, 3—בְּלֵב וָלֵב יְדַבֵּרוּ. " With a heart and a heart (double heart) do they speak." See also 1 Chron. 12, 33.

The Muhammedan and Hebrew codes agree also in this, that no corporeal punishments or pecuniary fines are imposed on those guilty of this dishonest practice, as is the case, for instance, with common theft. We have already seen that for stealing Muhammed enacts that the hands shall be cut off. And this very punishment was inflicted among the ancient Egyptians for the falsification of weights and measures. Also in the Hammurabi code we find this severe law concerning this matter :—

> § 108 :—" If a wine-seller has not received corn as the price of drink, but has received money by the great stone, and has made the price of drink less than the price of corn, that wine-seller one shall put her to account, and shall throw her into the river."

But in the Qorân, as in the Old Testament, men are taught to abstain from dishonest dealing lest they be deprived of God's blessing. So we read in Deut. 25, 15 :—

> " A perfect and just weight shalt thou have; a perfect and just measure shalt thou have; that thy days may be long upon the land which the Lord thy God giveth thee."

Baidawi in his commentary on the words in Sûra 83, which we have already quoted, refers to a tradition of Muhammed called خَمْسٌ بِخَمْسٍ,[1] in which the prophet says, " A people do not break a covenant without God giving the enemy power over them; and they do not give judgment contrary to what God reveals without poverty spreading among them; and wickedness does not appear among them without death spreading in their midst; and they do not give short weight without being deprived of the plants, and being overtaken with barren soil; and they do not keep back alms without the rain being held back from them."

[1] That is, " five by five," or retaliation, as, for instance, five punishments for five crimes.

At the present day, however, this, like many other crimes, is dealt with in Egypt, India, etc., by the ordinary courts of justice.[1]

(*e*) *Bribery*. There is only one direct reference made to bribery in the Qorân, namely, in Sûra 2, 184, where we read:—

> "Devour not your wealth among yourselves vainly, nor present it to the judges that ye may devour a part of the wealth of men unjustly, the while ye know."

In these words we have another example of the way in which Muhammed urged upon his followers the duty of dealing justly with each other. At the same time it seems somewhat strange that the prophet should give to this important matter, as he did also to that of theft, such scant attention. The space given to the subject in the Qorân by no means corresponds to the wide prevalence of the evil of bribery among the Muhammedans. On the other hand, it cannot be said that the matter is ignored by the Jewish legislators. For we find it referred to, and severely condemned, in several passages both in the Old Testament and the Talmud. On no account were the Jews allowed to take bribes. Thus Deut. 16, 19, says:—

> "Thou shalt not wrest judgement; thou shalt not respect persons: neither shalt thou take a gift;[2] for a gift doth blind the eyes of the wise, and pervert the words (cause) of the righteous."

Job 15, 34, reads:—

> "For the company of the godless shall be barren,
> And fire shall consume the tents of bribery."[3]

[1] See also Lane's "Modern Egyptians," chap. 4.

[2] שחד—A gift, esp. through which one buys off punishment. Ges. 14, H.W.B.

[3] See also 2 Chron. 19, 7; Ps. 26, 10; Prov. 6, 35; 17, 23; Isa. 1, 23; 33, 15; Am. 5, 12, etc.

In the Talmud (Keth. 105) the question is asked, "On what ground is the taking of a bribe forbidden?" As soon as a judge accepts a bribe from a party, he feels himself drawn to the same, and becomes as it were one person with the briber. But no one can examine what may be of disadvantage to himself. What, then, is the meaning of שׁוֹחַד?—שׁוּ־חד (=שהוא חד)? The judge is one with the plaintiff. Also, "The judge who accepts something from the other side is not competent to form a just decision."

One of the charges brought against the sons of Samuel was that of taking bribes; while their father, on the other hand, in his address to Israel could appeal to the fact that he had not been guilty of such practice.[1]

Thus has bribery at all times been regarded as a grievous sin, and rightly so, since its practice may lead to the most serious consequences both to the individual and the state. Among the Romans the corruption of a judge was reckoned among the crimes which were considered worthy of death. And had Muhammed given more notice to the matter in the Qorân, perhaps one would not find so much bribery in Muhammedan countries. The extent to which it is practised, for instance, in Egypt, is almost incredible. In general, says Lane,[2] the Naïb[3] and Mufti[4] take bribes, and the Kadi[5] receives from the Naïb. On some occasions, particularly in long litigations, bribes are given by each party, and the decision is awarded in favour of him who pays highest.

[1] 1 Sam. 8, 3; 12, 3. [2] "Modern Egyptians," chap. 4.

[3] نَائِب deputy. [4] مُفْتٍ teacher. [5] قَاضٍ judge.

G. LAWS CONCERNING FOOD, ETC.

1. *Food.*

It will not be necessary for us here to deal at length with the question concerning the ground or the grounds upon which primitive people distinguished between foods. We know that men from the earliest times have avoided certain kinds of herbs and of animals as food. While certain plants were instinctively avoided as being injurious to health or destructive to life, they had also a *horror naturalis*, that is, an inexplicable disgust, for many of the animals, and so avoided their flesh as unclean.[1]

On the other hand, W. R. Smith says,[2] " A prohibition to eat the flesh of an animal of a certain species, that has its ground not in natural loathing but in religious horror and reverence, implies that something divine is ascribed to every animal of the species. And what seems to us to be natural loathing often turns out, in the case of primitive peoples, to be based on a religious taboo, and to have its origin not in feelings of contemptuous disgust, but of reverential dread. Thus, for example, the disappearance of cannibalism is due to reverence, not to disgust, and in the first instance men only refused to eat their kindred." This author also refers to the fact that the Hebrew word ṭāmē is not the ordinary word for things physically foul, but is a ritual term, and corresponds exactly to the idea of taboo, which is found among all early peoples.[3]

[1] See Franz Delitzsch, " Comm. on Lev," chap. 11.

[2] " Kinship and Marriage," p. 308 f. See also his " O.T.J.C.," p. 366. Driver's " Deut." p. 164. Hastings, " D.B.," under the word " food."

[3] See Ges.[14] H.W.B. under טמא.

And as among other peoples, the Arabs also recognised this distinction of foods. While, however, blood and that which dies of itself are among the things that were generally avoided, yet some of the Arabs of the preislamic times ate both.[1] Sometimes blood would be drawn from a live animal, and poured into a gut, and then prepared on the fire.[2] This food was called *moswad*, and resembled our black-pudding.[3]

There are many references to the matter of food in the Qorân; and the following quotations will show that the enactments agree in general with those of the Old Testament.

> Sûra 2, 167 f. :—" O believers! eat of the good things wherewith we have provided you, and give thanks unto God if it be Him ye serve. He has only forbidden for you what is dead, and blood, and flesh of swine, and whatsoever has been consecrated to other than God.[4] But he who is forced, neither revolting nor transgressing, it shall be no

[1] " Abstemiousness from so many articles of food as are tabood by the Jewish Law naturally appeared strange to people whose supply was rather scanty, *and who did not* despise fallen camels."—Hirschfeld, " New Researches," p. 82.

[2] كان أهل الجاهليّة يصبونه فى الأمعاء ويشوونها—Baidawi.

[3] Lane (Lex. فَصَدَ) refers to a proverb which runs thus لَمْ يُحْرَمْ مَنْ فُصْدَ لَهُ—He has not been denied the entertainment of a guest for whom a camel has been bled by the splitting of a vein, and who has had the blood so obtained. The origin of the saying was this: Two men passed the night at the abode of an Arab of the desert, and, meeting in the morning, one of them asked his companion respecting the entertainment given by the host, and the latter answered, " I was not entertained as a guest, but only a vein (of a camel) was slit to draw blood for me," whereupon the other replied in the words above. Or a man used to entertain another as his guest in a time of scarcity, and, having no food to offer to him, and being unwilling to slaughter his camel, bled it by slitting a vein, and heated the blood that came forth, for his guest, until it became thick, and gave it to him to eat, hence the proverb.

[4] That is, such animals as are slaughtered without the words " *bismi 'llahi* " being uttered. But in this case one must not use the full expression " In the name of God, the merciful, the gracious," since they are not appropriate on such an occasion. Lane (" Modern Egyptians," chap. 3) says that some in Egypt, when about to kill an animal for food, say, " In the name of God! God is most great! God give thee patience to endure the affliction which he hath allotted thee."

crime in him. Verily God is forgiving and merciful."

The above words, with the following addition, are found in Sûra 5, 4:—

"And the strangled and the knocked down, and that which falls down, and the gored, and what wild beasts have eaten of—except what ye slaughter in time, and what is sacrificed to idols,[1] and dividing carcases by arrows."

Id. v. 6, reads:—

"They will ask thee what is lawful for them. Say, 'Lawful are those things which are good for you, and what ye have taught beasts of prey (to catch), training them like dogs, teaching them as God hath taught you. So eat of what they catch for you, and mention the name of God over it. . . . Lawful for you to-day are good things, and the food of those to whom the Book [2] has been given is lawful for you, and your food is lawful for them."

We will also give the following passages because they contain a further proof of Muhammed's acquaintance with the Jewish dietary law, and also show the light in which that law was regarded by him.

Sûra, 3, 87:—"All food was lawful to the Children of Israel save what Israel made unlawful to himself before that the law was revealed.[3]

Sûra 4, 158:—"And for the injustice of those who are Jews have we forbidden them good things which we had made lawful for them."

Also in Sûra 6 much is found on this subject; v. 147 reads:—

[1] Lit. "What is slain upon a stone." These anṣâb were certain stones which were placed around the Kaaba, over which when slaying an animal one used to utter the name of some God, and upon which it was the custom to slay an animal for the purpose of sacrificing it to some god or gods other than the true God.

[2] That is, Jews and Christians.

[3] Namely, the flesh and milk of camels (Baidawi). See also the note in Sale.

> "To those who were Jews did we prohibit everything that hath a solid hoof;[1] and of oxen and sheep did we prohibit to them the fat, save what the backs of both do bear, or the inwards, or what is mixed with bone. With that did we recompense them for their rebellion."

Further references to the matter will be found in Sûras 5, 6, 10, 16.

The above quotations show us that the prophet was well acquainted with the Jewish dietary laws. And according to Muhammed these laws were imposed upon the Jews on account of their iniquity. Still he did not find it possible, even if he desired, to abolish all distinctions, and to declare that every kind of food was equally clean and lawful to eat. Hirschfeld[2] regards all these passages that refer to the Jews as being late Medinan. If this view is correct, we see that they belong to a time when Muhammed had given up all hopes of being able to reconcile the Jews, and would, therefore, naturally welcome any new charge which he could hurl against his stubborn opponents. For, in most cases, he declares to be unlawful those things which are also prohibited by the Jewish code, as, for instance, that which had died of itself, blood, swine's flesh, etc.[3]

On the other hand, a Muhammedan is allowed to eat any of the above things when pressed by hunger. And in this the prophet follows the Jewish doctors, who grant the same liberty.[4] In Sûra 3, 44, Muhammed says :—

> "I confirm what is before you of the law, and make lawful for you some of that which was prohibited from you."

[1] On the words كلّ ذي ظفر Baidawi says, Everything which has a toe, such as a camel and cattle and a bird. And it is said to mean what has claws and hoofs. And الحافر (hoof) is called ظفر (claw) metaphorically.

[2] New Researches, p. 82.

[3] Cf. Lev. chaps. 7, 11, 17, 19; also Deut. chaps. 12, 14.

[4] Cf. Maimonides, "Hal. Melachim," chap. 8. § 1.

This means, says Baidawi, what was forbidden in the Mosaic code, such as the fat of animals,[1] fish, and the flesh of camels. As regards camels, Muhammed asks in Sûra 6, 145:—

> " And of camels one pair, and of oxen one pair (hath He given you)? Say: Hath He forbidden the two males or the two females, or what the wombs of the two females contain? Were ye witnesses when God ordained for you these?"

In this passage Muhammed endeavours to convince the Arabs of their superstitious folly in making it unlawful at one time to eat the males of these kinds of cattle, and at another time the females, and at another time again their young.

Again, as regards fish, it was permitted to them to eat only such as have no fins or scales. Sûra 5, 97, reads:—

> " Lawful for you is the game of the sea, and to eat thereof; a provision for you and for travellers."

Thus we find that while Muhammed forbids the eating of many things which are also forbidden in the Jewish code, on the other hand, he allows his followers to partake of some things contrary to the law of the Old Testament. Further, in agreement with the Talmud it is allowed to a Muhammedan when hard pressed by hunger to eat things which under other circumstances are forbidden.

2. *Wine, Games, Images.*

Before bringing my treatise to a close, it may be well to consider briefly Muhammed's teaching on the use of wine, games, and images. I shall first of all give a few quotations.

Sûra 2, 216:—They will ask thee about wine and games of chance; Say, ' In them both is sin and profit to men; but the sin of both is greater than the profit of the same.' "

[1] Cf. Lev. chaps. 7, v. 23 ff. It is said of the Jews in a tradition, " Fats have been forbidden to them, but they sell them, and devour the prices thereof."

Sûra 5, 92 f. :—" O believers, verily, wine and games and statues and divining arrows are only an abomination of Satan's work; therefore, avoid them, that haply ye may prosper. Satan only desires to place enmity and hatred between you by wine and games, and to turn you from the remembrance of God and from prayer; but will ye not desist, and obey God? "

But, on the other hand, wine is prepared for those who shall enter Paradise. So we read in Sûra 47, 16 :—

" A description of Paradise which is promised to the God-fearing. Therein are rivers of water which corrupt not, and rivers of milk whose taste changeth not, and rivers of wine delicious to those who drink."

As regards the word خَمْرٌ it is applied, not only to wine, but also to any intoxicating and fermented drink. And it is generally agreed that the word as used by Muhammed in the foregoing quotations is to be understood in this general sense. And as one proof of this it is said that خمر was forbidden by the prophet when there was not خمر of grapes in Medina, the beverages of the inhabitants being prepared from dates.[1]

Muhammed says, " In both (wine and games) is sin and profit to men." And so some maintain that excess only in these is forbidden. And although the majority of writers are of a different opinion, yet the followers of the prophet in no wise abstain from them.[2]

[1] خَمْرٌ *gen. fem. varius mascul.* Vinum (potissimum ex uvarum succo paratum); *tum quoque* Omnis potus inebrians. (*Sunt autem, quo contendant primitivam vocis significationem esse potus inebrians et inde nomen vini ex uvarum succo parati derivatum ; in oppido Medinae enim non exstitisse dicunt vinum ex uvis paratum, ita ut voce* خمر, *qua usus sit Muhammedes in interdicto, omnis potus inebrians intelligatur, necesse fiat.*) etc.—Freytag Lex. See also Lane's Lex. under خَمْرٌ.

[2] " Like all barbarians, the Arabs were fond enough of getting drunk, but wine was a foreign and costly luxury; and the opposition to its use found distinguished advocates before Mohammed."—W. Rob. Smith, " The Prophets of Israel," p. 388. Note 16.

Further, the word مَيْسِرٌ is said to include all games of chance, such as dice, cards, etc. But it is usually applied to a particular kind of game with arrows which was practised by the Arabs. Briefly the game was as follows: The participators bought a camel (on credit), which they slaughtered, and then divided into ten (or, according to some, into twenty-eight) portions. Each player had an arrow, upon which was cut a number of notches, which stood for so many portions of the camel. Three arrows, however, had no portions allotted to them, and the players to whom these arrows fell, had to pay for the camel, which was then divided among the poor.[1]

Our quotations show also that Muhammed forbade the use of images. It is possible that this refers to idols,[2] of whom the prophet says they could not create a fly, though they assembled together for the purpose.[3] Or, as others think, the reference may be to the carved pieces of wood, etc., which were used in the game of chess. From the connection in which the word is found in the foregoing quotation, this last explanation appears to me to be the correct one.

[1] See Sale, Prel. Dis. chap. 5. Lane's Lex. under مَيْسِر. Also "Septem Mu' allakat, Imru 'lqais" (Arnold) line 22: and A. Fischer, in "ZDMG." Band 58, 877 ff.

[2] See Baidawi on Sûra 5, 92 f.

[3] Sûra 22, 72.

APPENDICES

1. The Sunnites and Shi'ites

The Muhammedan world is divided into two great camps, the Sunnites and Shi'ites, within which are found different schools of law. And as frequent references are made in the course of the work to the teaching of these schools, it may be well to refer briefly here to their founders and their teaching.

The Sunnites are so-called from their reception of the "Sunna" or traditions as having authority concurrent with and supplementary to the Qorân. The Sh'ites are the partisans of the house of Ali. They reject the Authority of the Sunna, and believe that the Sovereign Imâmat, that is, the temporal and spiritual headship over the faithful, was by divine right vested in Ali and in his descendants, through Hasan and Hosein, the sons of Fatima, the daughter of the prophet, and, consequently, regard the first three Caliphs, Abu Bekr (A.D. 632–634), Omar (A.D. 634–643), and Othmân (A.D. 643–654) as usurpers. The Shi'ites are found chiefly in Persia and India, but the influence of their teaching has penetrated into other parts of the Muhammedan world.

The Sunnites, who are by far the more numerous (being about 20 to 1 of the Shi'ites), are divided among the following four orthodox schools, taken in the order of their numerical strength, Hanifees, Shâfiees, Mâlikees, Hanbalees, so called after the names of their respective founders. These four schools were established under the Abbaside Caliphs.[1]

[1] There were in all 37 Abbaside Caliphs, of whom Abu Jaafar, surnamed el-Mansur (A.D. 754–775), Harun-ar-Rashid (A.D. 786–809), and El-Mamun (A.D. 812–833) were the most celebrated. It was under the Abbasides that the power and glory of Islâm reached their highest point.

(*a*) Abu Hanîfa an-Nomân ibn Thâbit (A.D. 699–769), born at Kufa, was educated in the Shiʿa school of law, and received his first instruction in jurisprudence from Imâm Jâfer-i-Sâdik (the sixth Imâm of the house of Muhammed), whom he often quotes as his authority. Later Hanîfa seceded from the Shiʿa school, and founded a system of his own. Hanîfa is the main pillar of the deductive method, which undertook to create precedents in Muhammedan law by analogy, in agreement with the spirit of the Qorân, the traditions, and the decisions of the first four Caliphs. His system is the most followed of any.

(*b*) Abu Abdallah Muhammed ibn Idrîs ash-Shafeiʿ (A.D. 770–819) was born in Ghizah in Syria. From 783 he was under the instruction of Mâlik in Medina, and later was mixed up in a plot in Jemen, and was confined as prisoner in Bagdad. Here he became acquainted with the Hanîfee doctrine through ash-Shaibani. But since neither of the two prevailing doctrines satisfied him, he developed a new system himself, in which he lays special stress upon the methodical investigation of the foundation of the law.

(*c*) Abu Abdallah Mâlik ibn Ans (A.D. 705–795) was born in Medina. In contrast to the school of Hanîfa, Mâlik confined his teaching strictly to the traditions. His chief work was entitled Muwatta.

(*d*) Abu Abdallah Ahmed ash-Shaibani el-Marwâri ibn Hanbal (A.D. 780–855) was born in Bagdad. At twenty years of age he made a journey through Asia, that he might hear the chief teachers of the traditions. On his return to his own country he applied himself to the teaching of ash-Shafeiʿs until that scholar left for Egypt, when he himself appeared as a teacher. Refusing to acknowledge the Qorân to be created,[1] he was, by the

[1] The orthodox believe that the Qorân is uncreated and eternal. This question, however, was at one time the subject of a heated controversy. The Abbaside Caliph el-Mamun made an edict declaring the Qorân to be created. This edict was confirmed by his successors, Muʿtasim and Wâthik, who whipped, imprisoned, and put to death those who held otherwise. Mutawakhil (A.D. 847–861) revoked the edict, and put an end to the persecutions.

order of the Caliph el-Muʿtasim, severely scourged and cast into prison, where he remained seven years. The school of which he is the founder may be regarded as a kind of puritanism, which aims at restoring the primitive purity of religious observances.

Generally speaking, Central Asia, Northern India, and the Turks everywhere are Hanifees; Lower Egypt, Southern India, and the Malay Moslims are Shâfiees; Upper Egypt, and North Africa are Malikees, while the Hanbalees exist only in Central and Eastern Arabia.

The doctrines of these four doctors are essentially the same as regards the fundamental dogmas, though they differ from each other in the application of private judgment, and in the interpretation and exposition of the Qorân. They are also much given to disputing over unimportant trivialities, such as the correct method of ablution, the exact position at prayer, etc. While Abu Hanîfa allowed great liberty in the exercise of private judgment in the exposition of legal principles, it is almost entirely excluded by the other three: they are wholly governed by the force of precedents, and do not admit the validity of a recourse to analogical deductions, or of such an interpretation of the law whereby its spirit is adapted to the special circumstances of any particular case. Their followers are, accordingly, designated Ahl-ul-hadîs (traditionists par excellence).[1]

2. Qorân Commentaries

Soon after the death of the Prophet, certain Muhammedan scholars applied themselves to the exposition of the Qorân, and between those that have been already published, and what exist only in MS., it may be said that thousands exist, of which the majority belong to

[1] Brockelmann, "Die Litteraturen des Ostens," Bd. VI. Syed Ameer Ali, "The Personal Law of the Mahommedans." G. Sale, "Koran," Prel. Dis. sec. 8. F. F. Arbuthnot, "Arabic Authors." (William Heinemann, London, 1890), "The Mohammedan World of To-day" (Fleming H. Revell Co., London and Edinburgh, 1906).

the Sunnites. The following authors are among the best known and most widely read.

I. At-Tabari (A.D. 837–923). This is a very elaborate work, of which there is an almost complete copy in the vice-regal library at Cairo. Tabari, who was a great traveller, composed many works on history, poetry, grammar, and lexicography. His work on jurisprudence extends to several volumes, and his historical works stamp him as one of the most reliable of Arab historians. Gibbon aptly calls him the Livy of the Arabians. He died at Bagdad.

II. Zamakhshari (A.D. 1075–1144) was the author of another famous commentary on the Qorân. Some, however, regarded him as unsound on some points. With his great insight, and still greater subtlety, he was too apt to read his own scholastic ideas into the Qorân. His work was edited by Nassau-Lees, Calcutta, 1859.

III. Baidawi ("Nâsir el-dîn abu ul-Khair abdallah ibn Omar el-baidawi"). This is by far the best known of Qorân commentaries. It is little more than an abridgment of Zamakhshari's, and was undertaken by special request with a view to avoiding the latter's supposed heresies. The author, as the latter part of his name shows, belonged to the town of Baida in Persia, where he was Qâdi (judge). He died at Tabris A.D. 1286.

IV. Khalaf ibn Ahmed, ruler of Sakastan (Segistan, Sistan), was a protector of poets and of scholars, to whose number he is himself reckoned. Amongst other literary works, he caused a commentary on the Qorân, in one hundred volumes, to be prepared, this being the largest of the numerous books of this kind of which we have any information. He died A.D. 1008.

V. The Tafsir Galâlain is a small but very useful commentary on the Qorân, which I constantly consulted in the preparation of this work. The commentary, as the name Galâlain (dual) shows, was the work of two, father and son. It was begun by Galal ud-din us Suyuti (1445–1505), who was first a Qâdi at Suyut in Upper

Egypt, and later a professor at Cairo, and completed by his son, who also became a professor.

3. Polygamy in India

The Rev. T. W. Reese, Calvinistic Methodist Missionary in Sylhet, says in a letter to me: "With regard to Muhammedans in Sylhet and Cachar, all my experience goes to show that it is an extremely rare thing to find a man with more than one wife. I have met with one or two cases, but I am sure that not one per cent. of the people avail themselves of this privilege of the Qorân. Probably something like one in a thousand would more adequately represent it. And even in the few cases where polygamy is practised among them, it is generally due to the absence of any issue by the first wife, and sometimes by her inability, on account of physical disease or weakness, to perform the household duties. It may be that the provision laid down in the Qorân, that separate establishments should be kept up for each wife, has prevented, especially among the poorer people, the practice of polygamy. But the sentiment of the community is decidedly in favour of only one wife. I have always found, when told that a certain Muhammedan had more than one wife, that he was regarded with a certain amount of cynicism so far as his co-religionists were concerned. Concubinage among the wealthy is extensively practised, and also divorce. But among the poor, as these things involve money, their circumstances act as a sufficient preventative."

As regards the treatment of women and children, Mr. Reese says: "The Missionary is regarded as a more harmless species than the rest of mankind (European), with the result that I have seen thousands of women in the villages. The Muhammedan women and children appear to be treated with pretty much the same consideration as women and children in Hindu society. Boys among Hindus would certainly get better treatment, and the same thing holds good with regard to male children among the Muhammedans. At the same time, the Muhammedan women are more strictly secluded than their Hindu sisters, as is shown by the fact that it is a rare thing to find a Muhammedan Girls' School. Our Girls' Schools on the Plains are almost entirely composed of Hindus. In the Silchar school, with a roll number of 150, we have not a single Muhammedan girl, although a large percentage of the population is Muhammedan. The girls among the Muhammedans marry later than among the Hindus; the rule with the former being that marriage should take place after puberty is reached, while among the latter it should be an accomplished fact prior to that event."

4. Hallam and the Reformers

In a note, Vol. I. p. 68, Hallam says: "The notion of these divines . . . are not very consistent or intelligible. The Swiss reformers were in favour of the divorce, though they advised that the princess Mary should not be declared illegitimate. Luther seems to have inclined towards compromising the difference by the marriage of a secondary wife (Lingard, p. 172). Melanchthon, this writer says, was of the same opinion. Burnett, indeed, denies this; but it is rendered not improbable by the well-authenticated fact that these divines, together with Bucer, signed a permission to the landgrave of Hesse to take a wife or concubine, on account of the drunkenness and disagreeable person of his landgravine (Bossuet, "Hist. des Var. des Eng. Protest." Vol. 1, where the instrument is published). [Cranmer, it is just to say, remonstrated with Osiander on this permission, and on the general laxity of the Lutherans in matrimonial questions (Jenkins's edition, 1. 303).] [1]

[1] "The Constitutional History of England from the Accession of Henry VII to the Death of George II." By Henry Hallam, LL.D., London, John Murray, Albemarle Street, 1872.

5. The Hebrew Law of Divorce

On this subject the late Prof. Driver ("Comm. on Deut.," p. 272 f.) says: "Hebrew law . . . does not institute divorce, but tolerates it, in view of the imperfections of human nature (πρὸς τὴν σκληροκαρδίαν ὑμῶν, Mt. 19 [8]), and lays down regulations tending to limit it and preclude its abuse. Thus the law of Deut. provides *three* guarantees against rash or arbitrary divorce: a definite and substantial ground must be alleged; a proper legal instrument must be prepared; and the case (it is implied) must be brought before some public functionary, who would not only secure the due observance of the requisite legal formalities, but also take care that the grounds alleged were sufficient, and consider any defence that might be offered. The deed, moreover, in order that the divorce may be legally valid, must be delivered into the wife's hand, and she must be formally sent by her husband out of his house. It is evident that the time and expense involved in these formalities would tend to check a divorce suit being rashly instituted; the husband would have opportunity for reconsideration, and the intervention of a public magistrate would prevent proceedings being instituted upon wanton or frivolous grounds. The further provision in Deut. that a divorced woman who had married a second time should not return to her former husband, would operate similarly as a deterrent from hasty divorce, or, if the divorce had actually taken place, it would lead the husband to consider the possibility of taking his wife back, while he was still at liberty to do so, viz., before she had bound herself to a second husband; it would also be of value in a different direction by checking, on the part of a woman desirous of returning to her former home, the temptation to intrigue against her second husband. In two cases the right of divorce is withheld, viz., where a man slanders his newly-married wife as unchaste, or seduces her before marriage (22, [19, 29]), the ground, no doubt, being, in the former case, that a husband guilty of such a mean attempt to get rid of his wife deserved to forfeit the right altogether, and in the latter case, that a woman who had been so treated had a claim to special consideration at her husband's hands, and should not be exposed to the additional disgrace of a divorce."

I may also refer the reader to a valuable article by the Rev. Prof. Kirsopp Lake, D.D., Leiden, on "The Earliest Christian Teaching on Divorce," in the "Expositor" for Nov. 1910.

6. The Marriage Portion

Winckler ("Die Gesetze Hammurabis," p. 38, note 4) says: Es wird unterschieden: 1 tirḫatu, ursprünglich der Kaufpreis, den der Mann für die Frau zahlt; also der Mahlschatz, später aber in entgegengesetzter Entwicklung; Mitgift, das, was die Frau vom Vater mitbekommt; 2 Šeriḳtu, das Geschenk," die vom Vater der Frau gewährte Mitgift, die wohl als peculium angeschen wird (vgl. § 159 ff.); 3 nudunnû, das Geschenk des Mannes au die Frau (Morgengabe).

7. Murder and Theft in Egypt

In the letter already referred to, p. 10, after remarking that wilful murder is punished by hanging, and robbery by imprisonment, sometimes with hard labour, Mr. J. D. Bryan, Alexandria, says: "You see from the last two points that modern civilized methods have superseded the old *Sharia*ʻ. Ordinary crimes are dealt with by civil courts, and not by the Mekhemeh Shariaʻ. There is now no cutting off of hands and feet for theft, nor flogging or stoning for adultery. In theory no execution of a Moslem can take place without the sanction of the head of the religious court, but in practice, as in the notorious case of Wardani, who murdered the Prime Minister, the civil courts overrule the objections of the Grand Cadi, and carry out their judgment. Islâm is in

a most interesting state of transition. The old legal *fard* are falling into disuse; their political ideals are becoming dim, and even their religious beliefs are being shaken."

8. Literature

In addition to the various Lexicons and Dictionaries, the following are the works which have been chiefly consulted in the preparation of this treatise.

Ali, Syed Ameer, Moulvi, "The Personal Law of the Mahommedans." London, 1880.

Baidawi, "Commentary on the Qorân."

Bettany, G. T., "The World's Religions." London, 1890.

Brockelmann, Carl, "Geschichte der Arabischen Litteratur." 2 vols. Weimar, 1898. Berlin, 1902.

Fluegel, Gustavus, "Corani textus arabicus, Lipsiæ." 1834.

Galâlain, "Commentary on the Qorân." Cairo.

Geiger, Abraham, "Was hat Mohammed aus dem Judenthume aufgenommen?' Bonn, 1833.

Gibbon, Ed., "The Decline and Fall of the Roman Empire." (In "The Chandos Classics.")

Hirschfeld, Hartwig, "New Researches into the Composition and Exegesis of the Qoran." London, 1902.

Kasimirski, "Le Koran." Paris, 1844.

K. Krcsmárik, Johann, "Beiträge zur Beleuchtung des islamitischen Strafrechts" ("Zeitschr. d. D. Morgenl. Gesellsch." Vol. 58, 1904.)

La Beaume, Jules, "Le Koran analysé." Paris, 1878.

Lane, Edward William, "The Manners and Customs of the Modern Egyptians." Paisley, 1899.

—— "Selections from the Kur-an." London, 1843.

—— "Arabian Society in the Middle Ages," Edited by Stanley Lane-Poole. London, Chatto and Windus, 1883.

Margoliouth, D. S., "Mohammed and the Rise of Islam." The Knickerbocker Press, 1906.

Meissner, Bruno, "Beiträge zum Altbabylonischen Privatrecht." Leipzig, 1893.

"Mohammedan World of To-day." Fleming H. Revell Company, 1906.

Muir, William, " The Corân, Its Composition and Teaching." London, 1878.
—— " Mahomet and Islam," 3rd ed. Revised. London, The Religious Tract Society, 1895.
Müller, Dav. Heinr., " Die Gesetze Ḥammurabis und ihr Verhältnis zur mosaischen Gesetzgebung sowie zu den XII Tafeln." Wien, 1903.
Nöldeke, Theodor, " Geschichte des Qorâns." Göttingen, 1860.
—— " Sketches from Eastern History." London and Edinburgh (A. and C. Black), 1892.
Palmer, E. H., " The Qur'ân Translated " (" Sacred Books of the East." Vol. VI. IX.) Oxford, 1880.
Sachau, " Muh. Recht nach Schafiitischer Lehre."
Sale, George, " The Koran." Translation and Prel. Disc. (In " The Chandos Classics.")
Smith, R. Bosworth, " Mohammed and Mohammedanism." London, 1874.
Smith, W. Robertson, " Kinship and Marriage in Early Arabia." New ed. London, 1903.
Sprenger, A., " Das Leben und die Lehre des Moḥammad nach bisher grösstentheils unbenutzten Quellen." 3 vols. Berlin, 1861–1865.
Stobart, J. W. H., " Islam and its Founder." London, 1884.
Taylor, Charles, " Sayings of the Jewish Fathers." Second ed. Cambridge, 1897.
Ullmann, L., " Der Koran 9 Aufl. Bielefeld," 1897.
Wellhausen, J., " Ein Gemeinwesen ohne Obrigkeit," Göttingen, 1900.
Winckler, Hugo, " Die Gesetze Hammurabis," Leipzig, 1904.